RISE OF RUSSIA

GREAT AGES OF MAN

A History of the World's Cultures

RISE OF RUSSIA

by

ROBERT WALLACE

and

The Editors of TIME-LIFE BOOKS

TIME-LIFE BOOKS, ALEXANDRIA, VIRGINIA

Time-Life Books Inc.
is a wholly owned subsidiary of
TIME INCORPORATED

FOUNDER: Henry R. Luce 1898-1967

Editor-in-Chief: Hedley Donovan
Chairman of the Board: Andrew Heiskell
President: James R. Shepley
Vice Chairman: Roy E. Larsen
Corporate Editor: Ralph Graves

TIME-LIFE BOOKS INC.

MANAGING EDITOR: Jerry Korn
Executive Editor: David Maness
Assistant Managing Editors: Dale Brown, Martin Mann
Art Director: Sheldon Cotler
Chief of Research: Beatrice T. Dobie
Director of Photography: Melvin L. Scott
Senior Text Editors: Diana Hirsh, William Frankel
Assistant Art Director: Arnold C. Holeywell
Assistant Chief of Research: Myra Mangan

CHAIRMAN: Joan D. Manley
President: John D. McSweeney
Executive Vice President: Carl G. Jaeger
Executive Vice President: David J. Walsh
Vice President and Secretary: Paul R. Stewart
Treasurer and General Manager: John Steven Maxwell
Business Manager: Peter B. Barnes
Mail Order Sales Director: John L. Canova
Public Relations Director: Nicholas Benton

GREAT AGES OF MAN
Editorial Staff for *Rise of Russia:*
EDITOR: Russell Bourne
Assistant Editor: Carlotta Kerwin
Text Editor: Ethel Strainchamps
Picture Editor: Jean Tennant
Designer: Norman Snyder
Assistant Designer: Ladislav Svatos
Staff Writers: Sam Halper, Bryce Walker,
Edmund White, Peter Wood
Chief Researcher: Peggy Bushong
Researchers: Sue Massie, Alice Baker,
Irene Ertugrul, Rhea Padis, Ann Hersey,
Arlene Zuckerman
Art Associate: Anne Landry

EDITORIAL PRODUCTION
Production Editor: Douglas B. Graham
Assistant Production Editors:
Gennaro C. Esposito, Feliciano Madrid
Quality Director: Robert L. Young
Assistant Quality Director: James J. Cox
Copy Staff: Eleanore W. Karsten (chief),
Barbara Hults, Florence Keith, Pearl Sverdlin
Picture Department: Dolores A. Littles, Joan Lynch
Studio: Mervyn Clay
Traffic: Carmen McLellan

THE AUTHOR: Robert Wallace is a former staff writer for TIME-LIFE BOOKS. He has written numerous articles for LIFE, and is the author of *The World of Leonardo, The World of Rembrandt, The World of Van Gogh* and *The World of Bernini* in the TIME-LIFE Library of Art. He also wrote *The Grand Canyon* and *Hawaii* in the American Wilderness series. His work has been published in *Harper's, The Saturday Evening Post, The Reporter* and many other magazines. He has received the Sylvania Award for television drama and was presented the Newspaper Guild's Front Page Award in 1964 for the best magazine article published that year.

THE CONSULTING EDITOR: Leonard Kreiger, University Professor of History at the University of Chicago, was formerly Professor of History at Yale and Columbia Universities. Dr. Krieger is the author of *The German Idea of Freedom* and *The Politics of Discretion,* and is co-author of *History,* written in collaboration with John Higham and Felix Gilbert.

THE COVER: Shingled domes rise above the 18th Century Church of the Transfiguration, considered one of the finest examples of Russian wooden architecture.

The following departments and individuals of Time Inc. gave valuable aid in the preparation of this book: Editorial Production, Norman Airey; Library, Benjamin Lightman; Picture Collection, Doris O'Neil; Photographic Laboratory, George Karas; TIME-LIFE News Service, Murray J. Gart; Correspondents Peter Young and Felix Rozenthal (Moscow), Andrzej Glowacz (Cracow), Eva Stichova (Prague), Maria Vincenza Aloisi (Paris), Barbara Moir (London), Ann Natanson (Rome), Elisabeth Kraemer (Bonn) and Traudl Lessing (Vienna).

CONTENTS

INTRODUCTION

Our relations with the Soviet Union are of the greatest importance to American foreign policy today, and no fundamental part of that policy can be successfully maintained without the support of the American people. Therefore, the more Americans can learn about the Russian people the sounder our national policy will be.

To understand modern Russia, it is necessary to know something about the long history of the Russian people: today's Russian leaders are a product of that history, of the Russian experience and Russian tradition. Marxist ideology has been superimposed on that tradition.

While I was in the Soviet Union during World War II, the writer Aleksei Tolstoy, a distant relative of Leo Tolstoy, told me that to understand Stalin's Kremlin we must understand the Kremlin of Ivan the Terrible and Peter the Great. To understand those, we need to go back even further. This book brings nine centuries of Russian history vividly to life—from the Ninth Century Varangian Rurik, a half-legendary figure, to Peter the Great, a wholly real and wholly astonishing one.

Both as a private citizen and as an official of the government of the United States, I have had many opportunities over the past forty years to visit the Soviet Union on numerous occasions, to talk with successive Soviet leaders, and to observe the changes that have occurred in Russian life.

Today, the Soviet leaders are pragmatically adopting Western methods to solve the increasingly complex problems of production and distribution, as Peter the Great, in his own way, did before them. In addition, Stalin's concept of Communism as a monolithic structure has been shattered. Each of the Eastern European states is attempting to develop its own national policies, with greater independence from Moscow. Most dramatic is the conflict between Moscow and Peking—a conflict that is itself, in great part, a product of history and geography.

Perhaps the most intriguing change in the Soviet Union is the growth of a greater independence of thought. The illiteracy that existed when the Bolsheviks seized power has been almost entirely eliminated. Though the government still holds a tight rein on all forms of communication, more education has brought a demand for a freer access to knowledge and for greater freedom of expression.

In my opinion, this demand will be increasingly irresistible and will bring about many fundamental changes in the nature of Russian life.

Our own attitude toward Russia will affect the nature of those changes. Mr. Wallace's book should exert a most useful influence in this direction.

W. AVERELL HARRIMAN

A VIEW OF EARLY RUSSIA
ITS NATURAL REGIONS AND MAJOR CITIES

WHITE SEA

BALTIC SEA

ST. PETERSBURG

LAKE LADOGA

LAKE PEIPUS

NOVGOROD

SMOLENSK

POLOTSK

VLADIMIR-IN-VOLHYNIA

KIEV

CHERNIGOV

ATLANTIC OCEAN

CARPATHIAN MOUNTAINS

DNIEPER RIVER

CRIMEA

BLACK SEA

MEDITERRANEAN SEA

TUNDRA

BARENTS SEA

PECHORA RIVER

ARCHANGEL
NORTHERN DVINA RIVER

URAL MOUNTAINS

FOREST

LAKE ONEGA

OB RIVER

ROSTOV
SUZDAL
VLADIMIR

SIBIR

MOSCOW

KAZAN

NOVGOROD-SEVERSKY

STEPPE

VOLGA RIVER

URAL RIVER

DON RIVER

SARAY

ARAL SEA

CAUCASUS MOUNTAINS

ASTRAKHAN

DESERT

CASPIAN SEA

L+D DILLON

1

SWORDSMEN
AND SETTLERS

If the language and the spelling did not so clearly date them, the following comments about Russia could easily be passed off as having been made last week. "The state and form of government is plain tyrannical . . . You shall seldom see a Russe a traveller, except he be with some Ambassador or that he make a scape from his country . . . They are kept from travelling so they may learn nothing nor see the fashions of other countries . . . It may be doubted whither is greater—the cruelty or the intemperancy that is used in the country . . . As for the truth of his word, the Russe for the most part maketh small regard of it, so he may gain by a lie and breach of promise. And it may be said truely that from the great to the small the Russe neither believeth anything that another man speaketh, nor speaketh himself anything worthy to be believed."

These comments were in fact made by Sir Giles Fletcher, the English Ambassador to the Court of Fedor, son of Ivan the Terrible, in the years 1588-1590. Fletcher was not much concerned with analysis; he merely set down what he saw—or thought he saw—without relating it to the culture, character and history of the country. In fact he seemed almost to despair of fathoming such deep things, concluding in apparent frustration, "Russia, of all the countries of Christendom, differs so much from us. . . ."

Four centuries later it seems myopic, to say the least, to go on rephrasing Fletcher's observations and echoing his chauvinism without taking a more penetrating look at the Russian past.

The prospect may seem formidable. By far the largest of nations in expanse, Russia stretches nearly halfway around the earth; a single part of it, Siberia, is larger than the whole illuminated surface of the full moon. Within her borders, modern Russia contains more than 100 nationalities, the very names of many of which—the Adyghes and the Karachayevs, for example—are not merely unfamiliar to most people but are unheard of outside their native regions. The mention of some of the great figures in early Russian history—Yaroslav the Wise, Batu Khan, Boris Godunov, Alexander Nevsky—increases rather than lessens the sense of awe: the men are dimly known by name,

PUGNACIOUS NOMADS, *the Scythian warriors on the crest of this gold comb were among the first known inhabitants of Russia. Scythian horsemen swept in from Central Asia about 700 B.C. and pillaged Greek cities on the Black Sea. The comb was made for a Scythian chieftain by a Greek craftsman.*

but seem strange giants, cloaked in an "Asiatic" darkness that may be pierced only with the greatest of difficulty.

If the awe and the presuppositions are put aside, however, it becomes apparent that the history of Russia is neither as long nor as complex as that of most European nations. Russia's oldest surviving records date from the early 12th Century, and it has been only in the past 250 years that the nation has emerged from the Middle Ages. Long isolated from Western Europe, Russia grew up without participating in developments that many Russians, taking pride in their unique culture, find of dubious value. Russia was never a part of the Roman Empire. She never recognized the temporal or spiritual authority of the Roman pope. The Renaissance and the Reformation both passed her by; the scientific revolution was in Russia only a feeble reverberation of the explosion in the West. Her political and social revolution came so late that it seemed strange and frightening to more "sophisticated" nations who had experienced similar upheavals in earlier centuries. Russia is, as a result, the most unusual member of the European family—if indeed she is European at all; the question is still open to debate, particularly among the Russians themselves. Nonetheless, despite her ambiguous status and the varied origins of her peoples, Russia's history is essentially that of a single people, the Eastern Slavs. And despite her vastness, most of that history has been played out in an area not a great deal larger than the eastern United States.

Russia's history before the modern era is not well known in the West, and perhaps the least familiar of all is the story of her very early days—of the slow, agonizing struggle toward maturity that culminated in the reign of Peter the Great in the 18th Century. By the end of his life, Peter had forcibly Europeanized Russia, dragging her re-

SLAVS AND THEIR NEIGHBORS

▨ Extent of Slavic Peoples, 900 A.D.

THE SLAVIC FATHERS *of modern Russia settled the forest northeast of the Car-pathian Mountains. Other Slavic tribes migrated south and west to be-come Poles, Czechs, Croats and Serbs. Fierce nomads, who dominated the ancient invasion routes from Asia, hampered Slavic settlement of the steppe.*

luctantly into the "modern" world. By that time her national character had been largely formed; she was beginning to acquire the creative vigor and genius that would soon burst forth in her contributions to the literature, music and science of the world. She was about to become, in one word, adult. This latter, brilliant period in her life is familiar to most Westerners, but her early years remain a mystery, and in the story of those years may be found many keys to the riddles of her adult behavior.

Tremendous personalities and traumatic and unforeseen events helped to shape Russia's destiny. If the rise of Western Europe was characterized by continuity, that of Russia was quite the opposite—discontinuous, erratic, lurching. But it remains a remarkable and enthralling story, and among the early princes and the czars there are knights and villains enough for the most romantic taste. However, no single towering figure, not even Peter the Great, can truly be called the hero of Russia's youth. The "hero" is not one man but millions: the people themselves, whose spread into an empire and whose stolid survival in the face of all the woes brought on them by man and nature form some of the brightest chapters in the history of the human spirit.

Nature and geography have in many respects served Russia harshly. Seven eighths of modern Russia's vast bulk lies in the cold latitudes north of the line marking the United States-Canadian border. Because of Russia's climate, her agriculture has never flourished. The cold of Russian winter, however proverbial it is, cannot be overstressed. Fletcher wrote of it: "It would breede a frost in a man to look abroad at that time and see the winter face of that countries . . . Bears and wolves issue by troupes out of the woods. Rivers and all waters frozen up a yarde or more thicke, however swifte or broade they may be."

The bitterness of winter is not tempered, as it is in Western Europe, by the Gulf Stream. Nor are there any east-west mountain chains to prevent the ferocious winds from sweeping down from the Arctic Ocean deep into southern Russia. Other than in Siberia and along her southern borders, Russia has only one long range of mountains, the north-south line of the Urals, traditionally the line dividing Europe and Asia. But even the Urals are only ancient, worn-down hills, little more than 6,000 feet high.

Most of Russia is one enormous plain, once the floor of an ocean that stretched from the Arctic to the Black and Caspian Seas. This flatness has contributed much to the linguistic and cultural homogeneity of the country during its early development. In Western Europe the mountain ranges and valleys have nurtured innumerable dialects and varying folkways; in Russia, where there are few natural barriers to internal migration, the early culture—the language, art and religion—were national. The Russian plain has also facilitated the establishment and maintenance of a single political system, and has been of great importance in military history. Having few naturally defensible frontiers, Russians for centuries have relied on the principle of trading space for time—or in one historian's phrase, "defensive expansion." When they have been strong enough, they have occupied as much as possible of their flat borderland; under attack, they have fallen back across the plain, consolidating their forces in retreat.

As though in compensation for her cold climate and her monotonous landscape, Russia possesses one great natural asset, a magnificent system of interlocking rivers. Slow-moving and meandering, these rivers make communication possible in almost any direction across the great plain. As early as the Seventh Century A.D., traders and adventurers from Scandinavia, usually known as "Varangians," followed the Western Dvina and the Volga southeast to the Caspian Sea, sailed across it and proceeded overland to Baghdad. In the Eighth and Ninth Centuries active trade sprang up on the Dnieper, which empties into the Black Sea and thus made Byzantium readily accessible to northwest Europe, along a route famous as "the road from the Varangians to the Greeks."

Of the early inhabitants of the forested land of European Russia, there is little record earlier than the Ninth Century. It is known that they were Slavs—a linguistic rather than an ethnic term. They may have had an original homeland in the area northeast of the Carpathian Mountains between the Vistula and the Dnieper Rivers. A very prolific and, according to early, vague reports of them, a peaceful people, they were apparently driven out of their homeland by some unidentified invaders, around 500 A.D. The largest group of these migrants settled in what is now Russian territory, where in time they subdivided into three groups—the Great Russians, ordinarily called simply Russians; the Little Russians or Ukrainians; and the White Russians (perhaps so called originally because of their fair hair and complexion).

Once settled in Russia, Slavs rapidly occupied much of the forested land from the area of Kiev north and east to Moscow and Novgorod, driving out or absorbing the weaker Lithuanians and Finns in their path. The forest life was difficult in the extreme; against the crushing cold the Slavs built pit houses with low walls and with roofs rising only a few feet above the ground, mounded over with earth for insulation. Agriculture demanded prodigious labor—clearings were made with axes, and the felled trees were burned to provide fertilizer. After a few years the land was exhausted, so that the Slavs were constantly engaged in slashing and burning new areas of countryside, and at frequent intervals were compelled to move to a new location.

Although the Slavs were divided into large tribes, the basic social unit among them was only a rural community of a few score individuals related by blood or marriage, headed either by a patriarch or an elected chief. Property was held collectively, and important decisions affecting the group were taken in general council. Marriage by capture or purchase was common, as was polygamy. The religion of the Slavs was a complex mixture of many elements, including ancestor worship and animism. Idols were venerated, and there was widespread belief in Volos, the god of the dead, and Perun, the god of thunder and lightning.

The evidence of linguistics and archeology indicates that the early Eastern Slavs were familiar with the smelting of iron, obtained from deposits in the innumerable bogs in the woodland. They were also practiced in ceramics, weaving and various other household crafts, but in none were they particularly skilled. As farmers they were familiar with barley, wheat, apples, pears and a few vegetables, but the harsh environment of the cold forests kept their agricultural production to the level of their own immediate needs, and so they turned to trade. The forest provided some highly marketable products—rich furs, honey and beeswax. Scores of trading centers, many of them fortified towns, were built along the waterways, and by 800 A.D. the Slavs were beginning to send fleets of small craft southward. In Byzantium, or in the long-established Greek colonies on the northern shore of the Black Sea, the forest products were exchanged for cloth, wine, weapons and ornaments. Thus the Eastern Slavs in south-central Russia slowly began to achieve a measure of comfort and "civilization," although in the eyes of the sophisticated Greeks they remained only slightly more cultured than the barbarians.

A SLAVIC IDOL, *this nine-foot-high obelisk reflects early Russian pagan beliefs. The large figures at the top—probably sky gods, with a horse at the foot of one—dwarf the tiny men below. Underworld demons crouch at the idol's base.*

Wearying of the backbreaking labor in the thickets and bogs of the north, the Slavs must always have been strongly attracted to the broad steppe that lay south of them. Between the forest and the frozen tundra to the north was only the taiga, a soil belt even less productive than their own. But the soil of the steppe was rich and black, somewhat like that of the Canadian prairies. The open country offered no obstruction to the plow; the land was not only rich but beautiful. There is no detailed description of it dating from early times, but in the 19th Century the novelist Nikolai Gogol saw part of the steppe in pristine condition and wrote this about it in *Taras Bulba:* "In those years, the entire southern part of Russia, all the way to the Black Sea, was a green virgin wilderness. Never had a plow driven through the long waves of wild growth and only the horses, hidden in it as among the trees of the forest, trampled the tall grass. There could be nothing more beautiful in the world: the visible surface of the earth looked like a golden green ocean, its waves topped by multicolored spume. Through the tall, slender stems of the grass showed sky-blue, marine and purple star thistles; yellow broom thrust up its pyramidal head; the white parasols of Queen Anne's lace gleamed near an ear of wheat that had appeared there God knows how and was now growing heavy. Partridges scurried among the thin stalks of the steppe plants, and in the sky hawks hung immobile on their outspread wings, eyes glued on the ground. . . .

"In the evening, the steppe was completely transformed: the whole multicolored area caught the last bright reflection of the sun and then began to darken. . . . Fragrance from the plants increased— every flower, every blade of grass released its incense and the whole steppe was bathed in a wild, noble aroma. . . . The daytime music was replaced by a different one: spotted marmots crept out of

PRIMITIVE ROCK PICTURES, *some 3,000 years old, are evidence of early man in northern Russia. Water birds and a stylized ship indicate a people familiar with the sea. A fur-clad man, holding sun and moon symbols, and an elk suggest they were also hunters.*

their holes, rose on their hind legs and filled the steppe with their whistling. The whirr of grasshoppers gradually dominated other sounds. Sometimes like a silver trumpet, the cry of a swan reached them."

It would have been a natural development for the Slavs to occupy the steppe and cultivate it—as indeed they repeatedly attempted to do—but the steppe was a place of terror as well as beauty. Its flatness and the luxuriance of its grass made it a highroad of invasion by fierce, nomadic tribes from central and eastern Asia, who had been pouring into it since the dawn of history.

There were at least eight of these invasions in historical times. The earliest steppe nomads of whom there is any accurate record were the Scythians, who swarmed out of the east around 700 B.C. Herodotus, who spent some time in the Greek colony of Olbia on the north shore of the Black Sea two centuries later, observed them at first hand. In combat they were savage and efficient, fighting from the saddle with bows and short swords. When they were victorious, they made drinking cups from the skulls of their enemies.

The Scythians were overthrown by the Sarmatians, and the Sarmatians in their turn by the Huns. (The Huns did not stop when they reached the end of the steppe but, under their great leader Attila, they fought their way into the heart of France, and in 452 A.D. reached the very gates of Rome.)

Of all early Asiatic invaders, the Huns appear to have been the most dreadful, both in aspect and behavior. Broad-shouldered but with short, sticklike legs, they lived, ate and slept on horseback. The Roman historian Ammianus Marcellinus, who not only saw but fought them, wrote of "their horribly swarthy appearance. They have a sort of shapeless lump, if I may say so, not a face, and pinholes rather than eyes." The Huns, too, were soon displaced by later hordes sweeping out of Asia. In 558 came the Avars, large, powerful fighters who took pleasure in casual cruelty—it was their custom not to use horses or oxen to pull their wagons, but instead to yoke up four or five women.

On the track of the Avars came the Khazars, who were a more enlightened people than their predecessors, and who were more interested in trade than in plunder and butchery. The Khazar rulers, diplomatically evading a choice between the Christian and Islamic religions of their powerful neighbors, embraced Judaism. (Many Jews had migrated to the thriving Khazar trading cities during the time of persecution in Byzantium under Leo III, and had mingled as intellectual equals with the Khazar ruling class, who were tolerant of all religions.) The Khazars were in control of the steppe from the mid-Seventh Century to the early 10th, during the era when the first Slavic traders ventured south to the Black Sea. They permitted the Slavs to pass through their territory, extracting a

tax of about one tenth of their goods. Apparently they also allowed a limited number of Slavic plowmen to cultivate parts of the steppe, although they exacted a tribute. However, the relatively gentle Khazars were to remain the exception; other steppe nomads always repulsed the Slavs in bloody routs. The fierce Pechenegs succeeded the Khazars; the Polovtsy drove out the Pechenegs, and eventually the all-conquering Mongols were to take over the steppe as their base.

But perhaps by now at least a part of the reason for a Russian trait that foreigners have always regarded as xenophobia may be clear. For too long a time, in the past, Russian plowmen and princes alike squinted apprehensively toward the East, never knowing what new horror might come thundering down upon them. (Later they would look with equal anxiety toward the West.)

It is ironic that the steppe and the forest peoples should have been in such conflict in the early years, for their relationship would eventually become one of the closest interdependence. Neither can live without the other. The steppe requires the forest products and the manufactures of the north; and the north, without the grain provided by the steppe, would starve. But at the beginning of recorded Russian history, and for a considerable time thereafter, the separation was almost total.

It was in the mid-Ninth Century that the Slavs embarked on their long journey toward nationhood.

At that time they inhabited about a million square miles of forest land, roughly in the shape of an oval, with the Kiev-Novgorod line as its long axis. The people themselves, an amorphous mass numbering four or five million, were at first without political organization or even a sense of kinship from tribe to tribe; the only authority they recognized was the local chieftain. Under the circumstances they might easily have fallen under the domination of one of their neighboring states. To the east, along the middle Volga, was the kingdom of the Volga Bulgars, organized, formidable, and rapidly being converted to Islam. To the southeast, between the Caucasus Mountains and the lower Volga, was the benign but strong trading state of the Khazars. To the south was the Byzantine Empire, wealthier, more powerful and with a more impressive urban civilization than any other part of Christendom.

Yet it was not the Mohammedan Bulgars, nor the Jewish Khazars, nor the Christian Byzantines, any more than the Slavs themselves, who laid the foundations of the first Russian state. The impetus came out of the wild, pagan far north, in the form of wandering bands of Scandinavian warrior-traders who had no intention of founding a state at all.

These Scandinavians—more often called "Normans" or "Varangians" by the Russians—were brothers to the Vikings who ravaged England, France and Sicily. But instead of taking to the open ocean, they searched out the inland water routes from the Baltic to the Black Sea. Their interest was in obtaining wealth by the sword wherever possible, and by trade where it was not. Above all they sought access to the fabled riches of Byzantium, which they several times attacked.

As the Varangians proceeded southward along the Volkhov and Dnieper Rivers, they passed through the heartland of the Russian Slavs, and gradually brought it under their domination, either by insinuating themselves into the upper class of wealthy Slavic traders or by outright conquest—the Slavs were not militarily organized or well armed, having no weapons to match the heavy two-edged swords and battle-axes of the invaders. Typically, a Varangian prince would establish himself and his retinue of warriors in one of the major Slavic towns and take tribute from the surrounding territory, extracting a portion of the goods that the Slavs had been exporting to the south. The prince too would become a trader, and to protect his revenues he would build fortifications and defend his frontiers, but he had no interest in formal government. During the Ninth Century, strongholds on both sides of the waterway to Byzantium were set up by many Varangian princes, although there seems to have been little attempt at unification.

Traditionally, the dim beginnings of the first Russian state are traced to the year 862, when the Varangians were "invited" to rule over the Slavs. The information comes from the *Primary Chronicle*, the great, and indeed the only, Russian sourcebook of the early years. The *Primary Chronicle* is a monumental collection of religious, cultural, legal and historical material covering the period between the mid-Ninth and the early 12th Centuries. Its historical accuracy is somewhat open to question and its authorship is uncertain, but one version is supposed to have been compiled by Sylvester, Prior of St. Michael's Monastery in Kiev in the year 1116, who drew on oral tradition as well as written fragments.

According to the *Chronicle*, in the middle of the Ninth Century the Slavs wearied of domination by the Varangians and managed to eject them, but then fell into such quarrels among themselves that they decided to ask the Varangians to return to establish order. "They accordingly went overseas to the Varangian Russes: these particular Varangians are known as Russes, just as some are called Swedes, and others Normans, English and Gotlanders." In response, the Varangians sent leaders, and "on account of these Varangians, the district of Novgorod became known as the land of Rus." It was by extension, the chronicler suggests, that the whole country eventually became "Russia." (This explanation of the name by which their country is known in the West, it should be noted, is unacceptable to many Soviet officials; it piques their pride that their great nation should be named for a small band of greedy adventurers, and they have produced several competing etymologies of "Rus," but to little avail.)

The *Chronicle* records that the leader of the Varangian Russes was Rurik, a half-legendary figure who in 862 may have established himself at Novgorod. At about the same time, two other Varangians, Askold and Dir, seized control of Kiev far to the south. In 879 still another Norse prince, Oleg, brought both Novgorod and Kiev under his sway and laid down the basis of stable rule along the north-south waterway. Whether the *Chronicle*'s account of the "invitation" and of Rurik, Askold, Dir and Oleg is correct can never be determined; what is certain is that by one means or another a strong "Russian" leader had emerged in Kiev in the third quarter of the Ninth Century.

Kiev, because of its strategic location on the Dnieper, was the most important of all the towns of Rus. It was the southernmost fortified point in the forest region; just below it, in the town of Vitichev, flotillas of boats would assemble before mak-

THE FIRST RUSSIAN STATE *grew up around the great rivers that formed the main trade route between Scandinavia and Constantinople. Kiev, on the Dnieper River route, became its capital in 882.*

ing the run south through the dangerous steppe to the Black Sea. The ruler of Kiev, assuming leadership of the trading and military expeditions, also assumed a paramount political position; he took the title of Grand Prince while the chieftains of northern territories remained merely princes.

The style of rule established by the Kievan prince was simply an enlargement of the tribute system that had earlier existed on a smaller scale. With his more powerful army, Oleg could extort furs, slaves and other commodities not from small localities but from whole regions and cities—Novgorod, Smolensk, Chernigov, Rostov, Suzdal and others.

The rhythm of Russian life fell into a pattern of tribute-collecting and voyaging, as described by the Byzantine emperor-scholar Constantine Porphyrogenitus. During the winter, Slavs along the waterways built large boats, and when the ice melted in the spring, floated them down to Kiev. Meanwhile, Constantine wrote, "When the month of November begins, the chiefs together with all the Russians at once leave Kiev and go off on the *poliudie*, which means 'rounds,' that is, to the Slavonic regions of the [tribes of the] Vervians and Dregovichians and Krivichians and Severians and the rest of the Slavs who are tributaries of the Russians. There they are maintained throughout the winter (collecting 'taxes'), but then once more, starting from the month of April, when the ice on the Dnieper River melts, they come back to Kiev. They then pick up their boats, as has been said above, and fit them out, and come down to [Romania]." The trading voyage lasted until fall, when it was time to begin the cycle again.

By 907 Oleg was powerful enough to make a hostile rather than a commercial approach to Byzantium, and according to the *Chronicle* "accomplished much slaughter among the Greeks." His fleet of 2,000 boats was unable to enter the harbor, which was blocked by enormous chains, and so he "commanded his warriors to make wheels which they attached to the ships, and when the wind was favorable they spread the sails and bore down on the city from the open country. When the Greeks beheld this, they were afraid, and sending messengers to Oleg, they implored him not to destroy the city and offered to submit to such tribute as he should desire."

It seems probable that the writer of the *Chronicle* greatly exaggerated the terror in Byzantium, which the Slavs called Tsar'grad (the ruler's city). However, Oleg did manage to secure a trade treaty from the co-emperors Leo and Alexander. (Between the late Ninth and mid-11th Centuries Kievan rulers assaulted Byzantium six times; on each occasion the fighting was inconclusive and ended in a trade treaty.) The signatories of Oleg's treaty all bore Varangian names—Karl, Injald, Farulf, Gunnar, Frithleif. The roster indicates that the Norsemen were supreme in Kievan Russia at that time, but their dominance was temporary. Eventually the Slavs absorbed them almost without a trace, just as they would later absorb many other foreign elements. The last reference to "Varangians" in the *Chronicle* appears under the date 1054, and their cultural legacy was almost nil. It survives only in a few words or tales, such as the *Chronicle*'s account of Oleg's death.

According to the story, which seems to have been transplanted directly from Norse folklore, Oleg was warned by a sorcerer that his death would be caused by a particular horse in his stable. Oleg therefore never rode the horse, did not even approach it, but saw that it was well cared for. Ultimately the horse died, and Oleg "rode to the place where the bare bones and the skull lay. Dismounting from his horse, he laughed and remarked, 'So I was supposed to receive my death from this skull?' And he stamped upon the skull with his foot. But a serpent crawled forth from the skull and bit him on the

foot, so that in consequence he sickened and died."

How rapidly the Norse influence waned may be seen in the names of Oleg's successors—within two generations the grand prince of Kiev, though in the Varangian line, was called Svyatoslav; the last syllable tells the story. Svyatoslav, like Oleg, was a formidable warrior, and in a series of campaigns in the late 10th century he enormously expanded the dominion of Kiev. To the east he defeated the Volga Bulgars and sacked their capital, The Great Bulgar, which was situated near the present city of Ulyanovsk. He then broke the power of the Khazars on the steppe, turned westward to penetrate into the Balkans, and then southward to menace Byzantium. For a moment in history it appeared that he might establish a state of great size and power. However the time was not yet ripe, nor was Svyatoslav as clear in vision as he was strong in combat. In reducing the power of the Khazars, he opened the way for another host of westward-sweeping Asiatic nomads, the Pechenegs, and thus replaced a relatively mild neighbor with a savage one. In 972 the Pechenegs killed him and drank out of his skull, in accordance with the charming custom that had originated, according to Herodotus, among their predecessors, the Scythians.

The nature of Svyatoslav's loosely knit empire, moreover, was not such as to promote unity or durability. His rule was typically Varangian, based on the tribute system, with nothing to maintain it but force. There was no law higher than the sword; there were no common beliefs that might bind the Slavs together.

Svyatoslav's death brought the first, dim period of Russian history to a close. In the immediate future, far better documented than the past, the Kievan "state" would accept Christianity and literacy from Byzantium and would enter a period of greatness that rings like a far-off, golden chime in the memory of Russians to this day.

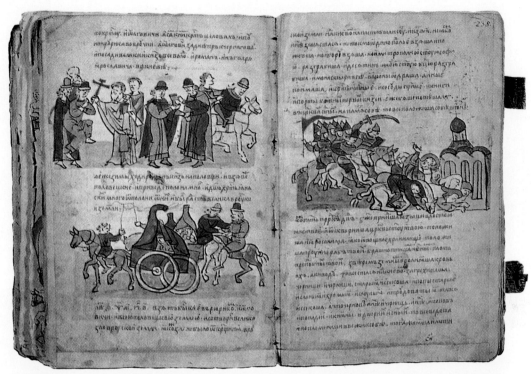

Two pages from the Radziwill Chronicle display the text and pictures that make it a national treasure.

"THE TALES OF BYGONE YEARS"

The legends of Russia's shadowy beginnings, along with the facts of her early history, are narrated in the *Primary Chronicle*, an extraordinary literary work with a lyrical introduction that begins: "These are the tales of bygone years . . . from whence arose the Russian land." The *Chronicle*, which tells about the nation's development from its mythical origins to 1110 A.D., was compiled by monks. The first draft was penned by an anonymous brother about 1037 A.D., and was emended and added to by others over a period of about 75 years. As Orthodox churchmen living in an incompletely Christianized land, the chroniclers intended some of their more horrendous accounts as cautionary tales, and into their blend of fact and legend they constantly inserted appeals to their warring princes to unite and live in brotherhood and harmony.

The *Primary Chronicle* is chiefly the story of the first Russian state, Kiev. In the 12th Century, Kiev broke up into independent principalities, each of which had its own annalists who used the *Primary Chronicle* as a part of their works. The text and illustrations reproduced here are from the Radziwill Chronicle, so called because it was at one time the property of Janusz Radziwill, a Polish prince, who acquired it from an unknown forester. It was written and charmingly illustrated by 15th Century monks, who added to the *Chronicle* narrative the stormy and colorful history to 1206 A.D. of their own Vladimir-Suzdal region.

лаже по велѣнїєсопатнѧмоу велнкой глоубокоу · ида во
рїстеремьскомъ внѣгра · и заоутра wлга седаше вне
ремѣ посла по гости · и прндоша кнгаще зовепѣ вышї
гла начть велнко · wни ирѣшамеъ де мко мь · ни на возѣхъ
понесети ны идой · рѣшлиснй мемамъ не вола · кнзьна
оубьенъ · ̈ аскнтннна хочѧ зашаше исмѧ · и понесошадло
и ина же седѧ в перегбе · в велнкн соустога горѧщеси
прнесошай в ла двор къ wлбѣ · несѧ чрнгоша
ʌмо слвею · и прнникше wлга ремѣ до бра ли вычесть
рѣша wнноу шины горе высмрти · иповелѣ заспа
тй ѧ жнвы · и ̈ засыпашлй ꙿ

Н послаи wлга к дерева ламо нрекн̈мъ · да аще мапросите пра
во · то прншлите мъ жа на рочиты · дабъ лицъ ни чти по
ида оу залаше исмѥъ · еда нпоу ста ме не лю испе вспе · се
слышаше дереваʌ не · нй збраша лоутни моу · н же держа
хоу дереваʌ скоую землю · и послаша по лю · дерева
но ми женї прнтешн · и повелѣ wлга мо въстро нт пре кще
суе измышепрннд кcомъ · wни претша нетьбоу
и влѣзоша дереваʌ не · нача мы тн · нца прошаш wнидаѧ

6453 / 945
Old Russian Modern

THE GREATEST EARLY RUSSIAN HEROINE WAS OLGA, WIFE OF IGOR, PRINCE OF KIEV. IN 945 A.D.—OR 6453 BY THE OLD RUSSIAN CALENDAR—IGOR WAS KILLED IN A BATTLE WITH THE DREVLIANIANS. THE VICTORS SENT EMISSARIES TO PERSUADE OLGA TO MARRY THEIR OWN RULER, AND TWICE SHE TRICKED THEM, INGENIOUSLY AVENGING HER HUSBAND'S DEATH. THE TALE IS TOLD IN OLD RUSSIAN (TRANSLATED AT RIGHT); OLGA IS SHOWN (LEFT) ORDERING THE BURIAL (ALIVE, BOAT AND ALL) OF THE FIRST ENVOYS. THE SECOND GROUP IS BEING BURNED ALIVE IN A BATH (ABOVE) AS OLGA SUPERVISES.

And Olga said to the Drevlianians: "Tomorrow I shall send for you, and you must say: 'We shall not go on horses, nor on foot, but carry us in our boat.' "And on the next day Olga sent for her guests. They sat in their boat with proud bearing and the servants brought them to Olga's palace. And they threw them, together with their boat, into a pit. And bending down toward the pit, Olga asked them: "Are you greatly honored?" They answered: "This is worse for us than Igor's death." And she ordered that they be buried alive. . . .

And Olga sent word to the Drevlianians: "If truly you ask that I marry your Prince, then send me your leading men, so that with great honor I may become the wife of your Prince." When the Drevlianians came, Olga ordered a bath to be prepared, saying: "After you have washed yourselves, then come before me." And they locked the bathhouse behind them and Olga ordered that it be set on fire at its doors. And so they all were burned.

6495 / 987
Old Russian / Modern

A nd Vladimir said to them: "Go first to the Bulgars and learn about their faith." They went and, arriving among the Bulgars, they saw how evilly things were done there and how they worshipped in the mosque, and they returned to their own land. And Vladimir said: "Go now to the Germans and see how it is with them also. And from there go to the Greeks." They went to the Germans and looked at their church service, and then they went to Constantinople and went to the Emperor. The Emperor asked them why they had come, and they told him all that had happened. When the Emperor had heard this he was glad, and sent word to the Patriarch, saying: "The Russians have come in order to learn about our faith. Prepare the church and the clergy, and you yourself put on your priestly robes, so that they may see the glory of our God."

Hearing this, the Patriarch ordered that the clergy be assembled; and according to custom they held a festival service, and they lit the censers and appointed the choirs to sing hymns. And the Emperor went with them into the church and placed them in an open place; and he showed them the beauty of the church, and the singing, and the serving of the arch-priest, and the serving of the deacons, and he told them about the service of his God. And they were in amazement and wondered greatly and praised the service. And the Emperor sent them forth with abundant gifts and in great honor.

RUSSIA OFFICIALLY BECAME A CHRISTIAN NATION IN 988, WITH THE CONVERSION OF VLADIMIR, RULER OF KIEV. THE RADZIWILL CHRONICLE CONTAINS A LEGENDARY ACCOUNT OF HOW THE CONVERSION CAME ABOUT. THE POWERFUL STATES SURROUNDING KIEV HAD ALL ADOPTED SOME FORM OF MONOTHEISM, AND VLADIMIR WAS WILLING TO ABANDON PAGANISM. BUT BEFORE COMMITTING HIMSELF, HE SENT ENVOYS ABROAD TO OBSERVE THE RITUALS OF THREE OF THE FAITHS. THE MEN WERE UNIMPRESSED WITH THE SERVICES THEY VIEWED IN ISLAMIC MOSQUES AND ROMAN CATHOLIC CHURCHES, BUT THEY WERE OVERWHELMED BY THE BEAUTY OF THE GREEK ORTHODOX RITES, DEPICTED BY THE CHRONICLE'S ILLUSTRATOR AT THE TOP OF THE OPPOSITE PAGE. THE ILLUSTRATION AT THE BOTTOM OF THE PAGE SHOWS THE ENVOYS MAKING THEIR REPORT. AFTERWARD, VLADIMIR CHOSE THE BYZANTINE FORM OF CHRISTIANITY AND DECREED THAT ALL HIS SUBJECTS BE BAPTIZED IN THAT FAITH.

ѿ красотоу црковноую · и пѣнья · и слоубы · а
рхиерѣискы · и престоиньед ѣисонъ · сказоую
ц еслоуженнеибгаство · ѡнижевыйгоумѣнни
быиши · иоуданыша · ипохвалишаслоубой и :·

И призвашай цр҃ь · василии · икостантинъ · р҃ёса
имъ · идѣтавземлюсвою · ипоустишаса дары
велими · ичтью · ѡнижеприидошавземлю · исозва
цр҃ьбоярыство · истарци · иреболомеръ · септнишапола
нинамилоу · даслыши ѿнибывшее · ирексакжи
те правдоу ожиною :·

лѣбъ къ юрьевьскому · въ то врема болно бѣ щю · и по
сла бра своего михалка · собравъ свои всеволодъ · поло
вцие · михалко же послуши мса · и въ ха борзо пои
и согони гмрѣкою бгомъ · собра рмдни и сторки · и по
е вадою своимъ володиславомъ · и поеха на дорогу
и поиѣкаша поро зепони · и усрѣтоша и с половою
и биша с ними · и одолѣша половщемъ бжьею помо
щью · и мны изъиша · а дрогиѧ избиша и дѣль въсе :–

рекоша изыманы · многолишаши на зади · переоша
мнозѣ нсоу · переводи нслѣ въ сдержа колдѧникисоу ·

After the Russians had adopted Christianity, their chroniclers saw God's hand in everything that befell the land. When the hostile Cumans, or Polovtsy, carried off Russian prisoners and livestock (top left), the chroniclers saw it as a divine punishment for past sins. And when an army set out from Kiev (lower left) and defeated the Cumans (the losers in the sword fight shown at right, below), the victory was taken as a sign that God's favor had returned.

In the winter the Cumans came to the Kiev side of the river and they captured many villages beyond Kiev, together with their people and cattle and horses, and they returned with much booty to the land of the Cumans. Gleb, Prince of Kiev, at that time being ill, sent his brother Mikhalko, together with his brother Vsevolod, to pursue the Cumans. Mikhalko, being obedient, went quickly after them and he overtook them beyond the River Bug. . . . And God helped Mikhalko and Vsevolod against the pagans. Some pagans they killed and others they took prisoner. And they took away from them their own prisoners, who were four hundred in number. They sent the prisoners back to their own lands, and they themselves returned to Kiev, praising God, and the Holy Mother of God, and the Holy Cross.

6683 / 1175
Old Russian / Modern

In the 12th Century, Vladimir-Suzdal had become the strongest principality to develop after the decline of Kiev. In 1175, according to the Chronicle, the boyars of the principality decided to do away with their grand prince, Andrei Bogolyubsky, who was unpopular because of his despotism and because of the fruitless wars he was always waging. One night some of the boyars, aided by Andrei's household manager, Anbal, entered Andrei's magnificent palace and murdered the prince. Taking advantage of the situation, a group of artisans and peasants started looting the palace and the prince's estates. The illustration depicts a hand-to-hand battle between the looters and the palace guard, in which some of the contestants are about to be killed.

When the night of Saturday had come the boyars seized their weapons, and like raging beasts they went to where the blessed Prince was lying in his bedchamber, and by force they broke down the doors. The blessed man jumped up and wished to seize his sword, but his sword was not there, for on that very day his steward Anbal had taken it away. And all rushing into his bedchamber, the accursed men slashed him with their sabers and swords and then went away. And he, in haste, ran after them and began to upbraid them and to speak in the agony of his heart. And they, hearing his voice, turned back to attack him again. He fled down the staircase, and there they found him and killed him. . . .

And the townspeople of Bogolyubovo plundered the Prince's palace, and the laborers who had come to work in the palace also did this, and much evil came about in the Prince's lands. They plundered the houses of his governors and overseers, and they killed his men-at-arms.

And Feodul, Abbot of the Monastery of the Holy Mother of God of Vladimir, went with the clergy and with the people to fetch the Prince, and they took his body on a Thursday, on the fifth day after his death. And they brought him to the monastery with honor and they laid him in the Church of the Holy Mother of God of the Golden Cupolas, wondrous and worthy of praise, which Andrei himself had built.

многоглаⷭ творивволостнего · посадникѣ · ити
оуновⸯѣ · домыпограбиша · асамыизбиша · идеⷭкые
имечникъиизбиша · адомыйпограбиша · невѣдоⷲгⷢаи
маго · адѣжезаконъ тоунивⸯиⷨ много · апакнапⷬⷪта
вⸯлагаⷮ · всⷨакⷬадⷲавⸯластиⷤповинⷣоеⷮ · естⷪложⷹ
мны · побеⷤⷣеⷮⷭⷯ кⷪмоⷤⷯчлкⷪцⷣ · властьюⷤесана
гⷭⷩовⷮ · вещавеликагⷪзлаоустеⷰ · тѣⷨжепротивⷣⷩ
волⷪⷭⷯти · противиⷮⷧ законⷪбⷤжью · икⷩⷥбонепⷪⷷⷩⷵе
мⷫⷩⷲⷯоⷭⷩ · бⷤьюⷤбослⷩⷥгаеⷮ : ~

омыиⷯⷫпренеⷰⷣⷮ вⷤⷯзратиⷨⷭⷯ · фейⷪⷧжениⷪⷩгоуменⷯ ·
стⷪⷷⷣецⷩⷫ воⷪⷧⷣдимⷩⷧⷯⷩ рⷩⷯⷭⷩⷪⷷⷭⷯⷭⷩⷪⷷ · сокрⷩⷯⷩⷧⷯⷩⷭⷯⷯⷣⷩⷯⷯⷩⷭⷩⷪⷷⷯⷩⷯ гⷩⷩⷧⷣⷩⷯ гⷪⷧⷩⷯⷭⷯⷩⷯⷩⷯⷩⷧⷩⷣⷩⷷⷯⷩⷩ
юⷩⷫⷣⷩⷷⷯⷩⷩⷷⷣⷯⷯ · исⷩⷩⷯⷫⷩⷣⷩⷯⷩⷷⷩⷯⷣⷯⷩⷯⷫⷩⷭⷩⷪⷷⷣⷩⷯ · рⷩⷩⷯⷫⷩⷩⷭⷩⷪⷷⷣⷩⷯ · вⷩⷯⷣⷯⷩⷯⷩⷯⷣⷯⷩⷩⷩⷭⷩⷪⷷⷩⷩⷷⷯⷩⷯⷩⷯⷩⷷⷩ
любⷩⷫⷣⷩⷯⷩⷩⷷⷣⷩⷯⷯⷩⷪⷷ · авⷩⷯⷫⷩⷣⷩⷩⷷⷩⷯⷩⷩⷭⷩⷪⷷⷣⷩⷯⷩⷯⷩⷯⷷⷯⷩ · паⷩⷯⷭⷩⷪⷷⷣⷩⷫⷯⷩⷯⷩⷷⷯⷩⷯⷩⷷⷩ
приⷩⷫⷯⷣⷩⷩⷷⷩⷯⷩⷯⷣⷩⷯⷩⷯⷩⷭⷩⷪⷷⷣⷩⷯⷩ · исⷩⷩⷯⷫⷩⷣⷩⷯⷩⷷⷩⷯⷣⷩⷯⷩⷯⷩⷯⷭⷩⷪⷷⷯⷩⷯⷩⷯⷩⷷⷯⷩ · иⷯⷩⷭⷩⷪⷷⷣⷩⷯⷩⷷⷯⷩⷯⷩⷷⷩ
вⷩⷯⷫⷩⷣⷩⷩⷷⷩⷯⷩⷯⷣⷩⷯⷩⷯⷩⷭⷩⷪⷷ · аⷯⷩⷭⷩⷪⷷⷣⷩⷯⷩⷷⷯⷩⷯⷩⷷⷩⷯⷩⷯⷩ
оⷩⷯⷫⷩⷣⷩⷩⷷⷩⷯⷩⷭⷩⷪⷷ
рⷩⷯⷫⷩⷣⷩⷩⷷⷩⷯⷩⷯⷩ
сⷩⷯⷫⷩⷣⷩⷩⷷⷩⷯⷩ

лⷩⷯⷫⷯ

2

THE ANCESTRAL STATE

If a date may be arbitrarily assigned to it, the golden age of Kievan Russia began in the year 980 when Vladimir, one of three sons of Svyatoslav, eliminated his brothers in a war of succession and became grand prince. One of the writers of the *Primary Chronicle*, a monkish soul who took an arithmetical interest in Vladimir's lecherous habits, noted that he was "overcome by his lust for women," had at least seven wives, and kept "three hundred concubines at Vÿshgorod, three hundred at Belgorod and two hundred at Berestovo." The chronicler also depicted Vladimir, at this stage in his life, as a cruel man and a pagan persecutor of the Christians, Jews and Mohammedans among the cosmopolitan population of Kiev.

However accurate this characterization is, Vladimir was an excellent soldier and administrator who was able to devote great energy to the enlargement and consolidation of his state. In the steppe to the south, which was controlled by the nomadic Pechenegs who stood athwart his trade route to Byzantium, he succeeded in pushing back the frontier to two full days' journey from Kiev, and he established strongly defended towns and lines of fortifications there. To the west he recaptured territories that had been seized by the Poles during the war of succession, and in the north he subdued the Lithuanians and took firm hold of a long section of the Baltic coast. By the year 1000, Kievan Russia was second in area only to the Holy Roman Empire among European political units. Its stability was tenuous, depending on the degree of loyalty that lesser princedoms would give to Kiev, but at least its five million people had begun to be drawn together into genuine nationhood.

Vladimir's great repute in Russia was not founded on his military or political success, however, but on his eventual acceptance of Christianity and his subsequent decree that all the people be baptized. According to the half-legendary account in the *Chronicle*, Vladimir was approached in 986 by representatives of various faiths who attempted to convert him. From the southeast came the Khazars, preaching the attractions of Judaism, but when Vladimir asked them why the Jews had been expelled from Jerusalem they could only reply, "God was angry at our forefathers, and scattered us

A PRINCE'S WAR HELMET *made of iron and silver bears the figure of St. Michael, the patron saint of princely warriors. The helmet was found at the site of a 13th Century battle between two brothers who were disputing a title. The inscription reads: "Archangel Michael, Help Fedor Your Slave."*

among the gentiles on account of our sins." Vladimir, who could see no promise in the faith of a dispersed people, sent them away.

From the east came the Volga Bulgars, hoping to persuade Vladimir to accept Islam. In the next world, they said, "Mahomet will give each man 70 fair women." That prospect may have appealed to the lusty Vladimir, but when the Mohammedans added that abstinence from wine was one of the conditions of their faith, he dismissed them with the famous remark, "Drinking is the joy of the Russes. We cannot exist without that pleasure."

Missions from the Roman and the Byzantine Churches met with greater approval in Vladimir's eyes—Christianity already had some standing in Kievan Russia and in Vladimir's own family; his grandmother Olga had been a convert. To assay the relative values of the Roman and Byzantine rites, Vladimir sent messengers who "beheld no glory" in the Roman Church as they observed it in Germany, but were overwhelmed by what they felt in the Cathedral of Hagia Sophia in Byzantium. "We knew not whether we were in heaven or on earth. For on earth there is no such splendor or such beauty, and we are at a loss to describe it." Thus the scales were tipped in favor of Byzantium, with the most profound consequences for Russia, and indeed for all of Europe.

Vladimir doubtless had reasons that the chronicler did not see fit to mention for abandoning paganism. At the close of the 10th Century, paganism in Europe was everywhere on the decline. The kings of Poland, Denmark, Norway and Hungary had all accepted Christianity within the preceding generation. Vladimir must have sensed that his political and commercial ambitions would best be served if he followed their lead. However, Roman Christianity, with its acceptance of the temporal authority of the pope, was not to Vladimir's taste. Byzantium might have attempted to exert some temporal authority as well, but before his conversion Vladimir took steps to avert this. He besieged and captured the Byzantine colony of Cherson in the Crimea, and then struck a complex bargain that involved his conversion, his marriage to the sister of the Byzantine co-emperors, and his return of Cherson as a token of friendship. His relationship with the hierarchy of Byzantium thus became that of an equal, certainly not of a vassal.

Vladimir, who was eventually to be canonized, came to be regarded in Russia as an evangelist with a charisma equal to the apostles'. Eulogizing him in the mid-11th Century, the Kievan Metropolitan Hilarion spoke of the Christian destiny of Russia in the proudest terms—"[our] church is a wonder to all surrounding lands, and so that the like cannot be found in all the northern land, nor in the east nor the west."

Vladimir plunged into his new faith with characteristic zest. He flung into the Dnieper the idol of the thunder-god Perun, with its silver head and gold moustache, and ordained that all the people, will they, nill they, be baptized. According to the *Chronicle*, he immediately reversed his wicked, pagan ways and became the model Christian prince— "He invited each beggar and poor man to come to the prince's palace and receive whatever he needed, both food and drink, and money from the treasury." He took Biblical injunctions humbly and literally, notably Christ's words "Resist not him that is evil," with the result that the countryside was soon overrun by bandits. Byzantine churchmen felt compelled to point out to him that a line had to be drawn somewhere, since he had been "appointed by God to chastise malefactors," and persuaded him to order some monitory executions. Nonetheless, in Vladimir's attitude, the warmth and quality of early-Russian Christianity may readily be sensed: he saw it as a gift joyfully to be received, not as a grim way of life.

Soon after his conversion Vladimir ordered the building of the first stone cathedral in Russia, the Kievan Church of the Tithe, completed in 996. Its title suggests the sincerity of his religious feeling —he assigned to the church one tenth of all his revenues, not only of those derived from Kiev but from all the tributary cities to the north, east and west. But Vladimir's manifest piety had small effect on the authoritarian attitude of the head of the Eastern Church, the Byzantine Patriarch, who did not wish to encourage religious nationalism in the newly converted state. The Patriarch took care to see that the head of the Russian Church—the Metropolitan—was under his control. During the 250 years that passed between the conversion and the submergence of Russia at the time of the Mongol invasion, only two Metropolitans were natives of the country; all the rest were Greeks. Russian princes were able to appoint some bishops and lesser officials, but many of those too were sent out from Byzantium.

Vladimir's insistence on the baptism of all the people met with considerable resistance; in some areas the rites had to be carried out at sword's point, and the mass of peasant, or "black-earth," people remained apathetic or downright pagan for generations. Long accustomed to ancestor worship and to orgiastic festivals, the peasants were not inclined to accept any form of Christianity, least of all the ideal of the humble, gentle Christ. Inflamed by sorcerers called *volkhvi*, they repeatedly rioted against the Church and they paid scant heed to such ex-cathedra denunciations as: "On Saturday evening men and women come together, play and dance shamelessly and indulge in obscenities on the night of the Holy Resurrection, just as ungodly pagans celebrating the feast of Dionysos; men and women together, like horses, frolic and neigh and make obscenities. . . . And now let them stop." The volkhvi continued to exert an influence

that may still be found, in remote, isolated rural areas, to this day.

The greatest response to Christianity came from the aristocrats of Kievan Russia, who embraced it with an enthusiasm equal to Vladimir's. In Christianity they found a sense of unity and purpose that had been lacking in their heathen days of random wandering and brutality. Their new religion gave them a sense of belonging to the civilized world and they eagerly welcomed all that Byzantium had to offer. Most important to their cultural progress was the establishment of a standardized literary language.

The Byzantine patriarchs had striven for more than a century to convert the Slavs. As early as the Ninth Century they had sent two scholarly monks, Cyril and Methodius, as missionaries to Moravia. These "apostles to the Slavs" are credited with devising two alphabets, both related to the Greek alphabet, in which they and their disciples transcribed the south Slavic dialect that they used in their mission. The dialect Cyril and Methodius used came to be called Church Slavonic because the first Slavic translations of the scriptures and other liturgical documents were written in it. (It was to become the base of literary Russian.) A modified form of Cyrillic, one of the alphabets they devised, remains in use in present-day Russia.

The establishment of Church Slavonic as Russia's liturgical language, however great a boon it may have been, had one unfortunate result. While it obviated the necessity of the Russian scholars' learning Greek or Latin, at the same time it cut them off from the classical heritage of the West.

The influence of Byzantine culture was dramatically evident in the arts, particularly icon-painting, religious frescoes and mosaics, and church architecture, which began to flourish in Kievan Russia after the year 1000. The Church also played a leading role in the widespread establishment of

almshouses, schools and monasteries; the last, as Russian history unfolded, were to have great importance in the colonization of the vast eastern frontier, serving as fortresses as well as religious centers. The earliest of these, the famous Monastery of the Caves, founded about 1025, still exists beside the Dnieper in Kiev. Down to the 20th Century its huge honeycomb of caves and tunnels could still be seen in the soft stone of the riverbank, together with the mummified remains of fanatical monks who had starved themselves in religious ecstasy, covering themselves with earth as they slowly died.

As he saw his own death approaching, Vladimir attempted to make the Kievan state politically stable by establishing family rule throughout his sprawling territory, setting up his sons as viceroys in the tributary cities. In Novgorod, for example, he placed his son Yaroslav, who was empowered to extract 3,000 grivnas from the city and its surrounding region, sending two thirds of the money south to Kiev and retaining the rest for local expenses. (The cash value of a grivna can no longer be determined; it was a small bar of precious metal of no permanently fixed weight. According to one widely accepted estimate, a grivna of Vladimir's day contained half a pound of silver. His revenues from all of Kievan Russia must therefore have been substantial.)

So long as Vladimir's sons remained loyal to him, the state remained fairly secure, and it might have continued to be stable if the sons had agreed on a system of succession after his death. However, that proved impossible—Yaroslav rebelled against him during his lifetime, and when Vladimir died in 1015 there ensued a fearful fratricidal war that was not settled for 21 years. In his heathen, polygamous days Vladimir had sired 12 sons who, having different mothers, shared little fraternal feeling. The details of their long struggle are of small in-terest today, except for the manner in which two of the younger princes, Boris and Gleb, met their deaths. Deeply imbued with the teachings of Jesus, they would not "resist evil with evil," refused to take up arms against their other brothers, and meekly submitted to assassination. They were later canonized, and for centuries have been fondly revered by their long-suffering countrymen. In 1036 the dispute over succession came to an end with the establishment of Yaroslav of Novgorod as ruler over all of Kievan Russia.

Under Yaroslav, called the Wise, the city-state reached its zenith. Yaroslav waged few wars, but in one supreme effort he crushed the Pechenegs on the steppe and removed them forever as a menace to the trade route to Byzantium. (As might have been expected, the elimination of the Pechenegs merely opened the way for a still more dangerous swarm of nomads, the Polovtsy, but these represented no great threat in Yaroslav's time.) In his conduct of foreign affairs he arranged a number of marriages that bound his family to the ruling houses of Western Europe. He was himself the husband of a princess of Sweden, and he married off three of his daughters to the kings of Norway, Hungary and France. A king of Poland married one of Yaroslav's sisters, and a prince of Byzantium another. In European eyes Kievan Russia was a great and enlightened state, already having a culture comparable to that of the West—Yaroslav's daughter Anna, having learned to write in Kiev, was able to sign her name to her marriage contract, whereas the bridegroom, Henry I of France, could only make an "X."

Emulating the emperors of Byzantium, Yaroslav built his own cathedral of St. Sophia, and decorated the passage that connected it to his palace with painted scenes of hunting, dancing and music. From the meager surviving contemporary written sources, it appears that Yaroslav had many skilled craftsmen at his command, among them potters, woodcarvers, goldsmiths, shipwrights, armorers, painters, bridgebuilders and stonemasons. There are no reliable population figures for the Kiev of Yaroslav's time, but historians believe it was as large as Paris, Europe's leading city, which had a population of about 80,000—twice as large as 11th Century London.

Yaroslav's name is closely associated with Russian law, which was first codified during his reign under the title of *Russkaya Pravda*—today the common meaning of *pravda* is "truth," but in earlier times the word also had the sense of "justice." Yaroslav's *Pravda*, compiled by the clergy, was based on Byzantine models adapted to traditional Slavic laws already in use in Kievan Russia, and is noteworthy in two regards; it was an exceptionally mild code by medieval standards, making the most sparing use of corporal or capital punishment, and it had a strong materialistic bias. The princes and merchants, in whose interest the law was primarily written, were more concerned with crimes against property than with crimes against persons. In a case of assault, for example, the punishment was only a small fine, but "if one sets fire to a barn, he is to be banished, and his house confiscated." The *Pravda* also contained much on loans and interest, which in the Kievan period often reached an annual rate of 40 per cent.

The structure of society in Kievan Russia was not feudal, as it was in Western Europe. Although the number of large landed estates increased as the Kievan period went on, there was also a free peasantry which was not bound to the land and could move about as it wished. Farmland could be bought, sold or bequeathed with little restriction, and there was no hierarchical system of fealty comparable to that in England and France. The mass enserfment of the population came at a later time, when serfdom was beginning to disappear elsewhere.

Kievan political institutions were of three kinds, autocratic, aristocratic and democratic, existing side by side in a curious and varying mixture. The autocratic was of course represented by the office of the local prince, whose prime responsibilities were in the administration of justice and defense of the frontiers. The aristocratic element consisted of a council of advisors to the prince called the *duma*. The chief military retainers of the prince were the original members of the duma, but eventually it came to include various administrators, wealthy merchants and important landholders, who were known collectively as *boyars*. Admission to the powerful boyar class, which for centuries was to play a major role in Russian history, was at first conditional on services rendered to the prince, although it later became hereditary as well. The boyar council was almost invariably consulted on important matters during the Kievan period, and it could occasionally veto the prince's suggestions. The democratic element was represented by the *veche*, or town assembly, which all free men could attend. In principle, any free man could convene the veche simply by ringing the municipal bell. Decisions of the veche, which ranged over all matters from petty private quarrels to the acceptance or expulsion of a prince, were required to be unanimous, with the result that veche meetings were frequently riotous and bloody.

The balance between the autocratic, aristocratic and democratic institutions varied from time to time and place to place. In Novgorod the veche was particularly strong; it hired its princes by contract, placed firm restrictions on them and ejected them if they failed in their duties. At one time, when the Grand Prince of Kiev wanted to place his son on the throne of Novgorod, the veche sent emissaries to him with a ringing, unequivocal message: "We were sent to you, O Prince, with positive instructions that our city does not want either you or your son. If your son has two heads, let him come." In other cities, according to their relative strength, princes or aristocracies were dominant, but the Novgorodian veche remained crustily independent from the 12th to the 15th Century.

The power of the boyar councils and the local assemblies of freemen worked against the unity of Kievan state, but there was a far stronger centrifugal force than these: the constant quarreling of an ever-increasing number of princes. Planning for his death, the great Yaroslav made an effort to ensure future harmony by setting up a system of succession as his father had done, dividing his realm into areas of diminishing importance. His oldest son received Kiev and Novgorod; his second son, Chernigov; and so on down to his fifth, who was established in the outlying region of Volhynia, to the west.

Yaroslav's apparent expectation was that his sons would die in the order of their birth; when the eldest died, each of the others would move up a notch, until at last the fifth son had the throne of Kiev. This system soon proved totally unworkable. Sons did not die in the proper order, and bitter arguments raged between sons and uncles— the son of the Prince of Chernigov, for example, could not inherit his father's throne, but had to give way to his father's first brother. To make matters worse the house of the Varangian, Rurik,

from which all the Kievan princes claimed descent, was extremely prolific. In time there were swarms of cousins, disputing their genealogical seniority and frequently resorting to the sword. Meanwhile the savage Polovtsy of the steppe, taking advantage of this clamorous disunion, fell upon the frontiers in yearly raids.

Kievan Russia did not, however, disintegrate in one calamitous quarrel. From time to time a truly great prince, capable of winning the affection and respect of the people, would arise, and there would be a resurgence of glory. Such a man was Vladimir Monomakh, a grandson of Yaroslav, who occupies in Russian history a place comparable to that of King Alfred in the English past. Vladimir Monomakh had all the attributes of the true chivalrous knight. When the Kievan veche offered him the throne he at first refused it, not wishing to violate the confused laws of succession, and he accepted it only when it appeared that otherwise the people would riot in his behalf and destroy the city. In 1101, 1103 and 1111 he led victorious campaigns against the Polovtsy, who until the coming of the Mongols were by far the most formidable force the Russians had to face. His lofty *Testament*, a manual of instruction for his sons, mentions 83 "long journeys," or battles, during which he killed 200 Polovetsian princes.

In the same document, Vladimir Monomakh cautions his sons against laziness, and reminds them to keep the fear of God in their hearts, to give alms generously, to free the oppressed, to judge the poor in person, and to give justice to the widow and or-

A FORTIFIED PALACE *was built by Vladimir Monomakh before he became prince of Kiev. Its wooden walls and towers, shown here in an artist's reconstruction, were destroyed by fire in 1147.*

phan. He then mentions a few of the many vicissitudes of his life: he has been twice tossed by bisons, gored by a stag, bitten by a bear and thrown to the ground by a wolf. "Children," concludes Vladimir Monomakh, "fear neither battle nor beast. Play the man. Nothing can hurt you unless God wills it. God's care is better than man's."

Unhappily Kievan Russia produced few great leaders after Vladimir Monomakh. The feuding not only continued but grew worse. In 1169 Kiev itself, "the mother of Russian cities," was captured and sacked—not by a foreign invader but by a Russian prince, Andrei Bogolyubsky. Andrei took the title of Grand Prince, but turned his back on Kiev and moved his capital northeast to a new city called Vladimir.

In scorning Kiev he merely acknowledged certain realities. The city had owed its importance to its strategic location on the north-south trade route. Byzantium had required that route because there had been one other way of exchanging goods with Europe—the more direct way, across the Mediterranean, had long been blocked by the corsairs of the Arabs. However, in the 11th and 12th Centuries the Arabian power had been reduced by Crusaders and by fighting merchants from Venice, with the result that Byzantine trade could flow directly west with small hindrance. "The road from the Varangians to the Greeks" was no longer important—nor, consequently, was Kiev. The Russians attempted to keep the waterway open, but as their incentive declined, so did their efforts. Ultimately the steppe nomads cut the route, and

with it they cut one of the great cords that had bound Kievan Russia together. No longer having a profitable common interest in trade, the princes turned to the cultivation of their lands; economic decentralization and parochialism became the rule.

As Kiev declined and the pressure of the steppe nomads increased, the population of the middle Dnieper began to migrate—in effect, Russia split into two parts that maintained only scant communication. One large group of migrants turned to the west and southwest—into Poland, the regions of Galicia and Volhynia—some journeying as far as the Carpathians whence the eastern Slavs had perhaps originally come. A larger group—the "Great Russians"—found their way into the forests of the northeast, between the upper Volga and the Oka rivers, which the raiding Polovtsy had not penetrated, and where, one day, the state of Muscovy would arise.

From its establishment under Vladimir to its collapse, the Kievan state had a period of greatness that endured at most for a century and a half; many scholars consider the time to have been even shorter. Nevertheless the Russians look back upon Kievan days with great nostalgia. In large part this is because of the spirit of optimism that pervaded the land in its early days. After their joyous acceptance of Christianity—with its handmaidens: a common language, law, the arts—the Russian aristocrats were filled with hopes for the greatness of their country. The common people as well, although for different reasons, had a sense of unity and purpose—or so, at any rate, runs the thesis of the greatest of Russian historians, V. O. Kluchevsky. In his phrase, Kievan Russia was "the birthplace of Russian nationality." The mass of people, observing the disunion of the princes and their frequent inability or unwillingness to establish order, realized that they must look to themselves, must find in their own strength the means to solve their problems. Thus, in Kluchevsky's words, "The inhabitant of Kiev was brought to think more and more of the dweller in Chernigov, and the dweller in Chernigov of the citizen of Novgorod, and all three of them of the Russian land." The phrase "Russian land," meaning not merely a territory but a motherland, appears everywhere in the chronicles of the time.

In their long, gallant and doomed fight against the invaders from the steppe—during which, thanklessly, they saved much of central Europe from devastation—the Russian people underwent a great ordeal, and it remains as a national memory that still evokes the highest pride.

Finally, there is something in the Kievan period that awakens a golden remembrance of chivalry as poignant as any in the West. Not all of the Russian princes were self-seeking, and not all the warriors were princes. There were many other bold fighters of lesser birth, "swaddled under trumpets, brought up under helmets, fed at the point of a lance," who went out year after year, generation after generation, to hold off the barbarians. The hopelessness of their cause is suggested in an epic tale of the time, in which the Russian warriors destroy the enemy with terrific blows of their swords, splitting them in half, only to find that each half becomes a whole warrior, until at the end the Russians are overborne.

As Kievan Russia disintegrated after the death of Vladimir Monomakh, the national sense of optimism was replaced by a pervading and increasing sense of gloom. The gloom was internally caused, but had the Russians been able to foresee events far to the east, their feeling would have been one not merely of gloom but of despair.

In the year 1206, unheralded, there took place in the region of Lake Baikal and the Gobi Desert an event of catastrophic portent. Mongolian tribes had long inhabited the area, fighting among themselves but posing no threat either to China or to the West. However, in 1206 one of the most important figures in world history, a tribal leader named Temuchin, gathered all the Mongols under his dominion and took the title of Genghis Khan. Five years later he broke through the Great Wall into China and, with an army of 100,000, conquered a nation of 100 million people. Genghis Khan then turned west with the intention of conquering the world. He sent his armies, swollen by the accumulation of countless Chinese engineers and technicians, through central Asia and into Persia. They passed south of the Caspian Sea, wheeled north and came up into the steppe through the Caucasian mountain passes. On the steppe they defeated the Polovtsy, who in desperation asked help from their old enemies, the Russians—"Today the Mongols have taken our land," said the Polovtsy, "and tomorrow they will take yours."

The Russians recognized the threat and many of the princes sent armies; a combined Russian-Polovetsian force met the Mongols on the banks of the Kalka River, a tributary of the Don, in 1223. At a crucial moment in the battle the Polovtsy broke and ran, leaving the Russian armies to be dismembered piecemeal. After the battle the victorious Mongols forced the leaders of their captives—several princes and knights—to lie on the ground while they built a large wooden platform over them. The Mongols then held a feast on the platform, crushing the Russians to death.

After their initial victory the Mongols ravaged Russia as far as the Dnieper but then suddenly withdrew to the east—they had internal political problems to settle, arising from the death of Genghis Khan in 1227. However, in 1237 they returned, led by Batu Khan, a grandson of Genghis, and the conquest of all Russia was soon effected.

The failure of the Russian princes to join forces contributed to their defeat, but it is doubtful whether any army in all history up to that time could have withstood the Mongols. They were superb horsemen, using both light and heavy cavalry formations; they had an excellent system of scouting and espionage, and they were equipped with heavy weapons taken over from the Chinese that could hurl wall-shattering boulders a distance of 300 yards. In open battle the Mongols placed auxiliary troops in the center of their line while the archers occupied the flanks. The center would fall back when charged, leaving the enemy open to crossfire from both sides. The Italian merchant-traveler Marco Polo, who later lived for 17 years among the Mongols, noted admiringly, "In this sort of warfare the adversary imagines he has gained a victory, when he has in fact lost the battle."

Although the Mongols respected courage in their enemies, they rarely showed mercy. They had been taught by Genghis Khan: "Regret is the fruit of pity." Divided into units of ten, a hundred and a thousand for easier control, their troops obeyed a discipline unmatched in its severity: if one or more members of a unit of ten was captured, the others were promptly executed after the battle.

At the head of about 150,000 such troops, Batu Khan in 1237 wiped out the kingdom of the Volga Bulgars, crossed the river, and started systematically reducing the Russian princedoms of the northeast. Within three years Batu rode north, west, south and east, conquering all but a single part of old Kievan Russia, defeating the Poles and Hungarians in central Europe, and reaching the shores of the Adriatic.

By 1242 Batu was ready for an assault on Western Europe, and that, from all indications, could scarcely have failed. The European kings and the Pope, like the Russian princes, were unable to present a united front against him. As Batu stood poised, however, word reached him that the Great Khan Ugedey, to whom Batu was subordinate, had

died in Mongolia. Accordingly Batu withdrew to the east, hoping to gain the supreme leadership for himself, and established his capital in the city of Saray on the lower Volga. Although the exact cause of Great Khan Ugedey's death is unknown, a papal legate, John of Plano Carpini, who visited his court, reported that the Khan had been poisoned by a woman in his entourage. If the account is correct, Western Europe owed its deliverance to some nameless, jealous woman who committed an opportune murder 5,000 miles away.

The Mongols posed no further threat to Western Europe except for occasional forays against German, Polish or Hungarian kings or princes who refused them tribute. They were apparently content with an empire which at its height, under Kubla Khan (founder of the Yuan Dynasty) included most of present-day Russia, Korea, all of China and Tibet, Syria, Mesopotamia, Turkey and parts of Persia.

The one great city of Russia that was not overrun by the Mongols was Novgorod, in the north—and the sparing of Novgorod was merely a matter of chance. Batu marched against it in 1238, but when he was within 70 miles of it a spring thaw turned the countryside into a swamp and he was forced to veer away to the south. It was inevitable that Novgorod's good fortune would come to an end—Batu or one of his successors could not have failed to bring the city under subjugation in time. However, when the assault upon Novgorod came, in 1240, it did not come from the pagan East but from the Christian West.

Since the time of the split between the Roman and Byzantine Churches in 1054, the pope had regarded the "heretics" or "schismatics" of the Eastern Church as little better than infidels, and when it appeared that the Novgorodians were engrossed with the Mongol threat, the Roman Catholic hierarchy did not oppose efforts to stir up a crusade against them. At the time Novgorod was no mere provincial city; it was a huge trading state, with territories in northern Russia extending from the Baltic to the Urals. Politically, with its powerful veche and its scorn of princes, it had a government as liberal as any that has ever taken root on Russian soil, although it would be misleading to call it a democracy. Novgorod may best be compared, perhaps, to some of the Italian city-states of the Renaissance, wherein freemen theoretically had the dominant voice but in fact were ruled by the aristocracy. In Novgorod the powerful boyar class supplied almost all the officials elected by the veche, and the boyars manipulated the veche by judicious choice of the issues presented to it. Nonetheless the Novgorodian government had in it strong elements of freedom; the people might have considered the recently signed English Magna Carta a rather backward document.

Along the Baltic the Novgorodians had three strong enemies—the pagan Lithuanians, the Catholic Swedes and the Teutonic Knights, a crusading order that had been organized in the Holy Land and later transferred to the region of present-day Prussia. The Swedes in July 1240 invested the mouth of the Neva River and attempted to block Novgorod's access to the sea. The 21-year-old Prince of Novgorod, Alexander, met them beside the river and crushed them, winning for himself the title "of the Neva," which immortalized him in Russian history as Alexander Nevsky.

In 1242 the Teutonic Knights, convinced of their mission to "Christianize" and Germanize Russia, marched against Novgorod and approached as close as Lake Peipus, where Alexander Nevsky took his stand. The battle was fought in April on the melting ice of the broad lake, and at first the Teutonic Knights had the best of it. Their heavily armored cavalry broke Nevsky's lines but in a brilliant flanking maneuver he obtained a tactical advantage and routed them, pursuing them for miles while the ice broke beneath them and hundreds drowned. In 1246 the Lithuanians, who might have profited from the examples of the Swedes and Germans, nonetheless attempted still another attack and were similarly routed by Nevsky.

Alexander Nevsky's victories were accomplished at a price—he knew that it was fruitless to take a stand against the Mongols, and so made peace with them, acknowledging their suzerainty, while he dealt with his Christian enemies. In 1242 he was forced to journey to Saray on the Volga and humble himself before Batu Khan. Batu agreed to permit Alexander to remain as prince of Novgorod, on condition that he pay tribute. Indeed, the Mongols were so impressed with Nevsky's courage that they later established him as titular Grand Prince of all Russia. Nevsky's choice between two evils, sometimes called "the Eastern option," appears in retrospect to have been the act of a realistic soldier-statesman, but the necessity of it still rankles in the Russian mind; few Russian historians can find a milder phrase than "a stab in the back" for the action of their Western fellow Christians.

The Novgorodians—who called their city "Lord Novgorod the Great"—did not easily acquiesce in Nevsky's agreement to pay tribute to the Mongols. With other townsfolk to the south, they refused to obey Batu's tax-gathering emissaries and drove them out. Nevsky foresaw that there would soon appear a Mongol army to devastate the land, and in 1263 he made another journey to Saray to plead for his people. He won them a reprieve, but died on the journey home. The Metropolitan of Russia uttered his obituary: "My dear children, know that the sun of Russia has set."

The sun had not in fact set, but it had surely been eclipsed. Russia was under the yoke that would bind the western part of the country for a century and the eastern part for two.

A CARVED LOG CHURCH, *built in the 14th Century, is a forerunner of the more flamboyant Church of the Transfiguration in the distance.*

A GENIUS FOR WOOD

For centuries woodcarving and wooden architecture provided the most direct and spontaneous expression of the Russian folk genius. Peasant homes were often elaborate products of the woodcutter's art—and they were filled with carved wooden furniture, kitchen utensils, toys and other objects. Even the simplest log chapels, like the one shown above, were carefully shaped by skilled axmen, fitted together and adorned with scalloped gables, toothed eaves and little shingled cupolas. And when these anonymous carpenters raised one of their cathedrals in the northern woods, like the remarkable Church of the Transfiguration on Kizhi Island, they produced the largest and most extravagant woodcarvings of all—veritable wedding cakes of intricately worked walls, gables, domes and spires.

NINE "ONION" DOMES *surmount a decorated octagonal drum of Our Lady of the Veil, a log church on Kizhi Island.* ORNATE SHINGLES, *fashioned out of*

SHINGLED MASTERPIECES

The Church of the Transfiguration, completed in 1714 on Kizhi Island in northern Russia's Lake Onega, was probably the most complex wooden structure the Russians ever erected. Yet, like many masterworks of its kind, it made use of astonishingly simple techniques. Working without a blueprint or a

poplar wood, sheathe the domes of the Church of the Transfiguration. The shape of the gables resembles a tall headdress women wore in medieval Russia.

surveying instrument, Kizhi's craftsmen built the elaborate church, with its 22 domes, "by the eye," as the Russians say. Not a single nail or other metal part was used; instead, the carpenters, who were experts in joinery, fastened the wooden parts together by notching them and interlocking them at ends and corners. Most remarkable of all, the only tool used in shaping the basic structure was an ax; saws, chisels and drills were used only for decorative details. So skillful did the carpenters of Kizhi's region become that they were recognized far and wide as Russia's finest craftsmen in wood.

THE SACRED SPLENDOR
OF GILDED WOOD

The interior of Kizhi's Church of the Transfiguration, like many early Russian Orthodox churches, glows with gilded carvings that tell the story of Christianity in intricate and reverent detail. Behind the main crucifix in the nave a carved partition called the iconostasis displays portraits of Biblical figures. Set into the iconostasis are three doors: in the center the Royal Door, seen in the photograph at right, is reserved for ordained churchmen and the czar; on either side are two small entrances used by altar boys and others assisting at the service. The whole iconostasis, along with other carvings and icons in the church, helped the illiterate parishioner to see at a glance the broad outlines of the Orthodox faith.

BAROQUE PLANT FORMS *adorn a column capital (above) and one of the sanctuary doors (left) in the Church of the Transfiguration. The intricately carved grapevine that covers the door is an elaboration of an ancient Christian motif.*

A WOODEN CRUCIFIX *portrays an emaciated Christ under a figure of God the Father, flanked by finely carved inscriptions and monograms.*

RUSSIA'S CHALET STYLE

During most of its history, Russia was a nation built of wood, and carpenters even spoke of "cutting" rather than "building" a town. Both rich and poor lived in wooden houses; only a few aspired to the grander stone or brick mansions preferred in Western Europe. Though most of the Kremlin in Moscow had been rebuilt of masonry by the 17th Century,

A LOG RAMP leads up to the hayloft of a peasant home. In such farmhouses the ground floor housed livestock, while the family carried on all its activities on the second and third floors. The logs were stripped of bark and left rounded on the outside but were cut flat on the interior. The details around the windows, seen in the closeup at right, reflect the influence of Western European styles: the S-shaped scrolls on top are baroque; the geometric designs below are local interpretations of neoclassical motifs.

Czar Michael continued to live in his wooden palace, convinced it was warmer and healthier than stone structures.

The prototype of all Russia's wooden construction was the peasant's home, of a style so simple that it could be erected within a few weeks. Logs were piled on top of one another until the house was the desired size (it might be as much as three stories high). Often the walls and roofs were finished before openings were cut for windows and doorways, which were then set off with carved trim and sometimes balconies. Within warm, spacious houses such as the north Russian chalet shown here, large patriarchal families of as many as 25 members could pass the winters in comfortable style.

TIME-HONORED PATTERNS

Carved motifs that go back hundreds of years are still to be seen on houses built along the Volga River. Many of these decorations echo designs first made for the bows of wooden river boats which have long since gone out of use. For centuries the craftsmen of the Volga region were celebrated throughout the country for building beautifully detailed vessels, and they frequently employed the same patterns of

flowers, fruit, birds and beasts to decorate household shutters, lintels and friezes such as those shown in the details on these pages. Two of the most ancient designs were a bushy-maned lion, seen at lower right, and the mythical siren above it, a sweet-singing bird with a woman's face, which since classical times is said to have lured mariners to their doom.

In preparing a panel for carving a craftsman first drew his design on a piece of paper and then placed the paper flat against the wood. Next he perforated the outline of the design with a needle and sprinkled the paper with coal dust, thereby stenciling the design in a pattern of dots onto the wood beneath. Finally he removed the paper and drew lines connecting the dots. After he had rounded out his design and added an extra flourish or two, he was at last ready to start carving.

A BEEHIVE, *carved in the image of a man, has hollow eyes and an open mouth to serve as entrances for the bees. Honey was removed from the back of the figure.*

A PEASANT HOME *contains wooden furniture and such utensils as a barrel for kitchen waste (left), a water bucket by the window, and behind it, a breadboard.*

A PAINTED MUG, *equipped with a hinged cover, held honey or beer. It was used in the south of Siberia.*

A DRINKING BOWL *(below) echoes a birdlike shape that first appeared within Russia as early as 2000 B.C.*

A PEASANT COUPLE *(left and above) are actually birdhouses. The birds entered through the faces and nested in the heads.*

HOMELY OBJECTS MADE INTO WORKS OF ART

In traditional Russia there were more woodworkers than craftsmen of any other kind. By necessity every peasant was a carpenter of sorts, and he often built his own house and furniture. In addition, itinerant professionals fashioned toys and furnishings for peasant homes. In their hands, everyday objects—wooden bowls, birdhouses, buckets, ladles—became original works of art.

The most ancient motifs used in Russian carving were geometric designs and stylized natural forms and religious figures. Peter the Great tried to Westernize Russian design by making it realistic, and during his reign craftsmen began to depict the world about them, including people in contemporary costumes. But, as can be seen in the 19th Century beehive and birdhouses illustrated here, the woodworkers continued to use the flair for bold forms and bright colors inherited from their ancestors.

SPINNING DISTAFFS, *arranged in three rows, display elaborate floral and geometric patterns and scenes from everyday Russian life. Women pulled carded tuft*

wool or flax through the multiple notches along the top of the carved and painted wood panels, then twisted the fibers between their fingers into yarn.

3

THE SCOURGE
FROM THE EAST

When the Mongols swept through Russia from 1237 to 1240, it was with a brutality that was almost beyond belief. A chronicler writing of their destruction of the large city of Riazan on the Oka River described nothing less than annihilation: "And they burned this holy city with all its beauty and wealth . . . and not one man remained alive. . . . All were dead. All had drunk the same bitter cup to the dregs. And there was not even anyone to mourn for the dead. And this happened for our sins." Great Kiev was so thoroughly gutted that barely 200 houses still stood, and the countryside for miles around was littered with human bones.

There was purpose in this horror. A nomadic people, the Mongols preferred the grassy steppe and had no wish to occupy the forested land to the north—nor had they, in fact, enough troops for such an undertaking. Accordingly, they reduced the Russians to a state of numb terror and then withdrew to the lower Volga where their army remained poised, somewhat like a spider on the perimeter of its web; if one of the stunned princely victims roused himself to defiance, the Mongols would dash out and destroy him. In the first century under the yoke, few princes dared to stir; only in southwestern Russia was there any serious attempt at resistance. Prince Daniel of Galicia went so far as to acknowledge the Roman Church and accept a papal crown, hoping thereby to secure Christian allies against the pagans, but none came to his aid, and the Mongols eventually brought him to his knees.

The Mongol stronghold on the steppe was known as the Golden Horde, not because it was the base of a swarm of yellow-skinned warriors, but because yellow was the imperial color of the khan and his clan. The name is believed to have come from an ancient Chinese system that assigned colors to the points of the compass: black was north, red was south, blue was east, white was west. Yellow, representing the center, became the imperial color. The word "horde" comes from the Mongolian *ordu*, meaning "camp."

From his administrative center Batu sent his tax collectors to all the Russian principalities that paid tribute or were, in the grim Mongol sense, "disciplined." The tribute was at first collected by means

A MONGOL HORSEMAN, *painted by a Chinese artist of the 14th Century, exemplifies the fierce spirit of the nomads who dominated Russia for 250 years. The Mongols, who conquered all of China and Central Asia before turning west, did all of their fighting and even ate and slept on horseback.*

of direct taxation, for which the Mongols had to take three censuses of Russia. (The last census, in 1275, indicated that the population was about 10 million.) The censuses were also used in military conscription; the Mongols dragooned innumerable men into their service, and there are records of Russian regiments serving as far from home as south China. The Mongol element in the Golden Horde was only a thin sprinkling at the top; beneath it, the great bulk consisted of volunteers from many central Asian tribes and conscripts from wherever they could be rounded up.

Although merciless in their exaction of tribute, the Mongols permitted the Russians to follow their own customs and laws, and were remarkably tolerant of the Church—the clergy paid no taxes on their large landholdings and were exempt from conscription. Batu and his lieutenants believed that all holy men, of whatever persuasion, should be left unmolested because their prayers might possibly be of posthumous benefit to the khans. Orthodox bishops, in return, prayed devoutly for their conquerors; a diocese was even established in the Golden Horde, and one of Batu's sons became a Christian, although most Mongols, by the middle of the 14th Century, had accepted Islam.

The Church during early Mongol times served much the same purpose that Alexander Nevsky had—it was the intercessor between the Russians and their oppressors. Of even greater importance was the role of the Church as the preserver of what remained of the great Kievan legacy and as almost the sole unifying force among a demoralized people. The mood of the Church was nonetheless penitential; its attitude was summed up in the chronicler's explanation of the destruction of Riazan: "This happened for our sins." Throughout Russia the Mongol terror was described from the pulpit as a deserved visitation of the wrath of God. The princes had sinned by their incessant quarreling, and the

people themselves had sinned in other ways—specifically, as Bishop Serapion of Vladimir put it, in "vile and cruel courts, bloody usury, and all sorts of robbery . . . adultery, vile speech, slander, perjury and calumny and other works of Satan." To ameliorate the God-sent punishment, Serapion prescribed meekness and charity: "Let us offer our love to God, shed tears, give alms to beggars according to our means; when able to assist the poor, let us rescue them from distress."

At first the Mongols sent out their own tax collectors, but then they turned the task over to the Russian princes. Each prince was obliged to journey to the capital of the Golden Horde at Saray—or occasionally to the headquarters of the Great Khan at Karakorum in Mongolia—to obtain a *yarlyk*, or charter. The yarlyk confirmed the prince as supreme in his territory, making him a viceroy of the khan, and was a document of high value. The possessors of yarlyks quickly discovered that, by squeezing their own people, they could extract even more tribute than the khans demanded and thus make a fine profit for themselves. At the court of the khans, competing princes tried to outbid each other for yarlyks, resorting to extremes of self-humiliation, bribery, treachery and violence. In their continuing feuds the princes also sought, and frequently got, the military aid of the Mongols against their own kinsmen.

The Mongol yoke was lifted slowly, first in western and southwestern Russia. The Mongols had never held firm and continuous control of the lands to the west of the Dnieper, although they had made devastating raids into the region, and after 1300 A.D. their power began to wane, leaving a vacuum that was filled not by the Russians but by their traditional enemies, the Poles and the Lithuanians. By 1350 the Poles had gained control of the rich principality of Galicia, and by 1400 the Lithuanians had carved out a huge grand duchy that extended

A MONGOL COIN, *inscribed with Arabic lettering, was found in western Russia. It was minted in 1403, some 50 years after the Mongols had been converted to Islam.*

from the Baltic almost to the Black Sea. In it were included the principalities of Kiev, Polotsk, Smolensk and Chernigov, and among its people were two of the three subgroups of the Eastern Slavs, the White Russians and the Ukrainians. (The third and largest subgroup, the Great Russian, was centered in the northeast in the region of the upper Volga.)

To be sure, the supplanting of Mongol by Lithuanian domination might appear to have been but a small relief, but this was not at all the case. The Lithuanians, though still pagan, were rapidly mellowing and they eagerly adopted Russian customs, culture and language. Russian princes and boyars were treated as equals, and intermarriage was common; the Orthodox Church was respected, and many of the Lithuanian nobility became converts. The White Russians and Ukrainians, who outnumbered the Lithuanians by perhaps three to one, were well content with their position; for all practical purposes, the Lithuanian state was really Russian. In the centuries to follow, this Russian-Lithuanian state would struggle with Moscow for ascendancy over the whole Russian land, in what was in effect a civil war between the southwestern and northwestern halves of the country.

Although the Ukrainians and White Russians gained their liberation after little more than a century, the Great Russians remained under the Mongol yoke for many years thereafter, until Moscow—or Muscovy, as the entire state came to be called—became powerful enough to throw it off.

There were reasons why the leadership of Great Russia should have fallen to Moscow, and not to any of several older, larger and stronger principalities. In part, the Muscovite rise to power was rooted in the "appanage" system—the years of Mongol domination are in fact generally known as the Appanage Period. The word refers to a grant of land given by a prince to one of his younger sons;

in Russia, where the custom of primogeniture was not followed, it became common in Mongol times for princes to divide their estates into as many appanages as they had male children. Thus, in each generation, the holdings of the princelings became progressively smaller, until finally there were numerous minor princes who possessed less land than the boyars, and not a few who had none at all.

With the division of the country into countless appanages, the parochialism increased—each minor prince focused his attention on his own small holding and took little interest in those around him. In such a situation it was possible for a single strongwilled individual or family to swallow up neighboring territories, and this is precisely what occurred in Moscow. The Muscovite princes did not ignore the appanage practice, but they followed it in a calculated manner; each prince left the major share of his estate to his eldest son, and only scraps to the others. Because the eldest could dominate his juniors and even take their lands from them if they disobeyed or displeased him, the Muscovite system was primogenitive in fact, if not in name. In addition to its shrewdly conceived inheritance system, Moscow had other great if undeveloped advantages. The small city lay directly in the path of the migration of the Great Russians from the middle Dnieper to the northeast, and it was ideally situated as a center of communication and trade. Its location on the Moscow River gave it ready access to the headwaters of four greater rivers, the Dnieper, the Volga, the Don and the Oka.

At the time of the Mongol invasion Moscow was one of the most insignificant principalities in the northeast, probably no larger than 500 square miles. It was dwarfed in importance by such surrounding centers of power as Rostov, Riazan, Vladimir and Tver, and it was minuscule in comparison with the huge city-state Lord Novgorod the Great. Indeed, Moscow was considered of such slight significance that when Alexander Nevsky died in 1263 he left it to the youngest of all his sons, Daniel. Apparently having much of his father's courage, if not his gallantry, Daniel attacked the neighboring appanage of Kolomna and added it to his own. He made other territorial acquisitions along the Moscow River, inherited another appanage from a childless relative, and passed his enlarged domain on to his son.

In Daniel's line there were several descendants of similar ability and acquisitiveness, among them Ivan I, called "Kalita," or "Money Bag." Ivan I collaborated closely with the Mongols, so ingratiating himself that he was rewarded with the designation of Grand Prince and the warrant to collect taxes in much of the Mongol-dominated area of Russia. With his profits he bought more land, snatching a village here and an appanage there, until he had increased Daniel's legacy fivefold. The relative peace and stability of his reign attracted many migrants to the Moscow region, and to increase the population still further (land was of no use without peasants to work it) he ransomed slaves from the Mongols and settled them in his principality.

The tranquillity and burgeoning power of Moscow under Ivan I also led to one of the most important of all events in the early history of the city: the Metropolitan of Russia, who had previously resided in Vladimir, transferred his see to Moscow in 1328. From that time forward the interests of the Church and the Muscovite state became closely intertwined, with the metropolitans unfailingly supporting the princes' drive toward dominance in the Great-Russian area. The metropolitans did not hesitate to employ the weapon of excommunication against the enemies of Moscow, and at times took an active part in the management of the state.

By 1378 Moscow had become strong enough to dare challenge the Mongols in battle; in that year Grand Prince Dimitry defeated a small Mongol army

and refused to pay the customary tribute. Determined to reassert their authority, the rulers of the Golden Horde formed an alliance with Lithuania, and in 1380 rode north. Their plan was to join the Lithuanians on the upper Don and, together with them, destroy Dimitry.

According to their deplorable custom, the other Russian princes might have been expected to offer Dimitry no help, but on this occasion almost all the major principalities sent troops, and an army of at least 150,000 was amassed. Of great importance in rallying the Russians was the Church—Moscow was now the spiritual capital of the northeastern lands —and the exhortations of the bishops lent Dimitry's cause something of the character of a religious crusade. With the Church's blessing, Dimitry's army went forth against 200,000 Mongol-led troops, and by good fortune caught up with them before they could join the Lithuanians.

In the historic battle of Kulikovo Pole (Snipes' Field), at the juncture of the Don and the Nepryadva Rivers, the Mongols were routed and sent reeling back to the Golden Horde. The cost to the Russians was great—only 40,000 able-bodied survivors were left, and Dimitry himself was found half dead among a pile of corpses, his armor shattered and pounded in. Nonetheless, the Lithuanians, hearing of the Mongol defeat, chose not to face the remnant of Dimitry's army and retreated to the west.

The victory of Grand Prince Dimitry, thereafter called Dimitry Donskoy (of the Don), was scarcely decisive; within two years another Mongol army had ravaged Moscow while Dimitry was recruiting troops in the north, and again clamped down the yoke. On his return to the ruined city Dimitry found 24,000 corpses in the streets; he paid for their burial from his own purse. Still the memory of Kulikovo lodged deeply in the minds of the Russians; Dimitry, by his demonstrating that the

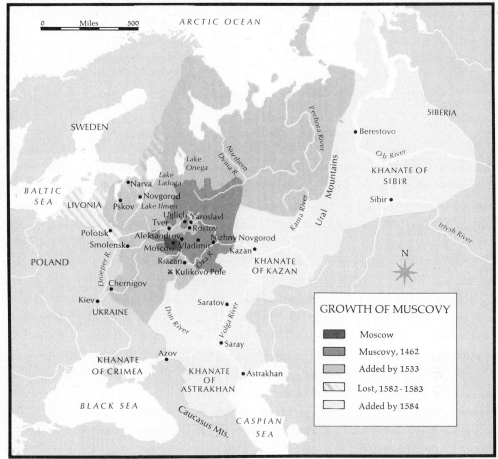

TERRITORIAL ACQUISITION *made the principality of Moscow into a great nation. Ivan III, who inherited Muscovy in 1462, and his son Vasily added lands to the north, west and south. Ivan IV doubled the nation's size with military campaigns to the east.*

GROWTH OF MUSCOVY

- Moscow
- Muscovy, 1462
- Added by 1533
- Lost, 1582-1583
- Added by 1584

Mongols could indeed be beaten, came to be regarded as not only a local but a national hero, thus adding still more to the prestige of Moscow.

If the Mongols had sustained the ferocity and drive of Batu Khan, they would doubtless have wiped out Moscow and killed Dimitry. But after 150 years of unchallenged power, the Mongols themselves had begun to be infected with the old Russian ill—disunion. The Great Khan in Mongolia had lost control of his subordinates, and the Golden Horde, now autonomous, was wracked by internal quarrels. Dimitry was allowed by the Mongols to remain as Grand Prince and thus to continue the Muscovite "gathering of Russia." While the territorial consolidation continued, the Golden Horde was attacked and beaten on the Volga by the greatest of Asiatic conquerors since Genghis Khan—Timur the Lame, known in the West as Tamerlane. Tamerlane, whose empire at its height included central Asia, all of the Middle East, the Caucasus and parts of India, pressed on into Russia after his victory over the Golden Horde and in 1395 at-

tacked the principality of Riazan, which was less than 150 miles southeast of Moscow. But then, for some reason, he turned back—possibly because he had learned of the Russians' extensive preparations to defend Moscow and of the strength of their army. The Russians themselves believed that they had been aided by divine intervention: a popular icon, Our Lady of Vladimir, had been brought to Moscow to help protect the city as Tamerlane's forces approached it; on the day the icon arrived, Tamerlane ordered the retreat. Whatever his reasons, Tamerlane disappeared from the Russian scene as quickly as he had come.

The Golden Horde revived briefly after Tamerlane's withdrawal, but in the first half of the 15th Century its power began a steady decline. Vasily I, Dimitry's successor, no longer paid the full tribute, sending "gifts" instead. Vasily might have thrown off the yoke altogether, but he was preoccupied with enlarging his state to the west and wished to placate the Horde while he did so. During his long reign (1389-1425) he fought continually against

Lithuania, recovering some small territories that had once been part of old Kievan Russia, and against the neighboring principality of Tver, which stubbornly refused to recognize the supremacy of Moscow.

Mongol domination was not dramatically broken in the northeast; it disintegrated as the Golden Horde slowly fell into fragments. A separate khanate was established in the Crimea in 1430, and others soon emerged in Kazan and Sibir along the southern and eastern Russian frontiers. In 1452 Moscow was able to reverse the roles of vassalage —a number of Mongol nobles took service with the Grand Prince, and one of them was rewarded by being assigned the small, subject principality of Kazimov. In 1480 there occurred an odd stalemate in which the armies of Muscovy and the Horde faced each other for weeks on opposite sides of the Ugra River, each afraid to attack the other. At length the armies fled in opposite directions, and formal Mongol dominance ended. However, scattered bands of Mongols and other nomads continued to harry the eastern frontier for centuries, and it was not until 1783 that the last powerful khanate, the one in the Crimea, was subdued.

What permanent effect the 250 years of Mongol domination had on the Russian people can only be a matter for speculation. The Mongols contributed almost nothing of cultural value—they were, as Pushkin later described them, "Arabs without Aristotle or algebra," and they are in no way to be compared with the brilliant Moors who occupied Spain. Indeed the Mongols actively retarded the growth of Russian culture by blocking the stimulus from Byzantium and the West; conceivably, had it not been for the Mongols, Russia might have participated in the Renaissance. However, living apart from the Russians in the main, the Mongols did permit them to develop their own culture.

As for the Mongol effect on the Russian social order, it was calamitous. The gropings toward freedom and democracy and the fairness and mildness of the legal code that had marked the Kievan state were wiped out. Russian rulers gradually came to resemble the khans in their harshness and despotism, either through imitation or through the necessity of paying them tribute. Despotism and enserfment, the two key facts of all subsequent Russian history, began under Mongol rule.

The Mongol disintegration coincided with the reign of Ivan III (1462-1505), called the Great. There are varying accounts of his character, but he seems to have been a cautious and somewhat devious man who "always took two bites at a cherry," who preferred to send his troops into battle rather than lead them, and who was said to be frightened of the dark. However, Ivan III had the same shrewdness and acquisitiveness that had characterized most of his predecessors. Under Ivan the Great, the "gathering" proceeded at a remarkable pace—by cash purchase, inheritance, treaties made under duress, and war. The largest of Ivan's acquisitions was the city-state of Lord Novgorod the Great, which included thousands of square miles in the wilderness of the north and northeast, beyond the Volga, in addition to its great capital city on the waterway leading to the Baltic. From the sparsely populated wilderness Novgorod got the principal items of its thriving trade, wax and furs, which were exported to the cities of the Hanseatic League to the west. Ivan doubtless cast his covetous eye on the wealth of furs; and that, coupled with a consuming desire to unite all of Russia under his own control, made the downfall and ultimate absorption of Novgorod inevitable.

The Muscovite Grand Princes had menaced Novgorod for many years before Ivan's time, and there had been considerable, though haphazard, infiltration and colonization of the Novgorodian territories in the northeast. In the American wilderness the Church customarily followed in the wake of trappers, traders and plowmen, but on the Russian frontier it was frequently the Church that led and the others that followed. This was particularly true in Mongol times when penitent monks, convinced that the Mongols had come "because of our sins," retreated into the wilderness to found monasteries where they might recover their pristine Christianity through prayer and hard labor.

The mother of Russian frontier monasteries was one called the Holy Trinity, established in the forest north of Moscow in 1340 by Sergius of Radonezh, who gave his blessing to Grand Prince Dimitry before Kulikovo and later became the most revered of all Russian saints. From the Holy Trinity-St. Sergius monastery, dozens of monks went forth into the Novgorodian territories to establish their own religious centers, several of which, being fortified, soon attracted frontiersmen who were neither Christian nor penitent. Some came simply to seize and cultivate small parcels of land; some were outlaws, fleeing the oppression of boyars and princes; the majority were lured by the riches to be obtained in furs: for two sable skins a peasant could buy a cabin and horses and the other livestock he needed.

The movement into the wilderness had not been planned or directed by the state; it was simply a spontaneous surging of the people, who won an empire almost by inadvertence. Moscow quickly acknowledged the movement, of course, and soon established a bureaucracy to collect taxes and administer law. But the distances were too great for communication, and the people too ruggedly independent to bother with the letter of Muscovite orders. In any case, when Ivan the Great embarked on his imperial mission Novgorod had already lost control of much of the hinterland. There was some doubt as to who did control it, but in the main the sympathies of the frontiersmen lay with Moscow, not Novgorod.

Novgorod's fall to Muscovy was precipitous and dramatic. *In extremis* Novgorod appealed for help to Lithuania; little was forthcoming. The upshot was that Novgorod surrendered, and Ivan soon did away with its independent institutions. "The *veche* bell in my patrimony in Novgorod shall not be; a *posadnik* (an elected mayor) there shall not be; and I shall rule the entire state." Ivan's bald announcement clearly indicated how far the ambitions of the Muscovite princes had gone—the democratic veche, the town assembly, was intolerable to him, and the word "patrimony" made plain that he no longer considered Novgorod (or any other territory where Russian was spoken or where Russians had once lived) outside his rightful jurisdiction. The veche was dissolved and its bell carted off to Moscow, and Ivan found an effective means of dealing with the Novgorodian boyars who opposed him: he deported them to areas remote from their homeland, initiating a practice that later czars and Communist officials would find very useful.

Ivan the Great turned next upon Tver, a major principality centered on the present city of Kalinin some 100 miles northwest of Moscow, and with equal ruthlessness conquered it in 1485. From Lithuania he seized all or parts of the old Kievan princedoms of Chernigov, Polotsk and Smolensk; in all, by the end of his reign he increased the domain of Muscovy to 55,000 square miles, a veritable empire compared to the 500 square miles inherited by Prince Daniel from Alexander Nevsky 250 years earlier. When Ivan had completed his territorial aggrandizement he had all of Great Russia under his effective control, with the exception of a few small regions later seized by his son.

Ivan's huge state was far closer to true nationhood than Kievan Russia had ever been. It contained a homogeneous people, united in religion and language and drawn together by their long experience of suffering under the Mongols. It is true that Kievan Russia had known similar unifying forces, and that nationalism ("the Russian land") had its beginnings there, but Muscovy had advantages that were unknown in earlier times. The Kievan state had consisted of several principalities loosely tied together; now all Great Russian principalities had been brought under a single head, within boundaries that coincided with linguistic and ethnographic dividing lines. The princes in Kievan times had warred among themselves, perpetuating disunion in the state; but with power centralized in Moscow, Russia's wars and belligerent confrontations were all with foreign powers and served to unite the state. It was no longer Kiev against Novgorod, or Chernigov against Smolensk, but all of them, with Moscow, against the outside world.

Muscovy was almost encircled by enemies—the Mongol khanates in the east and south, Poland and Lithuania in the west, the Teutonic Knights and Sweden in the northwest—and when one of them pressed inward, Muscovy became more solidly united.

The consolidation of Muscovy under Ivan the Great was a triumph of persistence and organizational skill, beyond all doubt the most important development in Russian history to that time. By no means all of the Great Russian people were pleased with it, but on the surface it was a triumph indeed. However, two things were still lacking: a sense of cultural self-confidence and a sense of the legitimacy of Muscovy among nations.

Despite the Mongols, Russians were at least aware of the wonders of the West—Ivan himself was a contemporary of Michelangelo and Leonardo—and in earlier times Russians had felt awed and uncouth in great Byzantium. As to the legitimacy of Muscovite status, not only abroad but at home,

Ivan and his boyars and clergy were proud, hypersensitive men who felt the need of doctrines and trappings that would make them appear not as upstarts but as the equals (or the superiors) of any others on earth. Thus, even as he gathered his realm, Ivan was also gathering some legitimizing ideas, with the eager cooperation of the Church. To some, their efforts may seem vainglorious and pathetic—but this is a viewpoint that comes more easily to those whose ancestors did not have to spend a thousand years fighting off nomads.

Ivan's first step, in 1572, was to marry Sophia Paleologus, a niece of Constantine XI, the last Byzantine emperor, who had died fighting on the wall of his city when it fell to the Turks in 1453. The marriage made Ivan, or so he assumed, the rightful heir of empire. To his family crest he added a two-headed eagle, the Byzantine version of the eagles that had been carried at the head of the Roman legions, and to his several titles he added "czar" and "autocrat." He borrowed the latter title from the Byzantine emperors, who had assumed it to indicate that, like the Roman emperors, they were supreme by divine right as well as politically. Ivan was moving toward complete autocracy, but he still had to reckon with the power of his boyars.

In further aggrandizing himself, Ivan, under his wife's tutelage, instituted a ponderous system of courtly procedure that foreign ambassadors found stupefying in its tedium and vanity. This self-glorification, common enough in emerging nations, was calculated to humiliate outsiders and thus to supply Ivan with the self-confidence he lacked. One of the earliest ambassadors to the Muscovite court, Count Sigismund von Herberstein, left an account of his own experience there that may bring a smile of recognition to diplomats of today. Herberstein, who represented the Holy Roman (German) Emperor Maximilian, first visited Moscow in 1517 during the reign of Vasily III, Ivan's son.

WEARING PADDED ARMOR, *Muscovite boyars of the 16th Century adopted this winter wear from their Mongol conquerors. The Russian princes also learned to emulate their Eastern overlords in the oppression of their subjects.*

He found the Russians obsessed with the Oriental matter of "face"—he was asked to dismount from his horse before greeting a boyar, who remained mounted. (Herberstein would have none of that; he dawdled in his stirrups and tricked the Russian into dismounting first.) In Moscow Herberstein and his companions found themselves sequestered: they could not go into the markets to buy food; it was delivered to them. The supply was ample, but the living quarters left something to be desired: there were no beds, and it was only after proper negotiations that Herberstein got some.

When at length Herberstein was admitted to the presence of the Czar, he was required to sit through a long period of imperial silence, during which he studied a silver basin at the Czar's elbow. The basin was filled with water in which the Czar ostentatiously washed his hands after greeting Herberstein—an unclean, Roman Catholic Westerner. At dinner the Czar served roast swan, plums and an inordinate amount of drink. Afterward Herberstein was sent back to his quarters, accompanied by Russian noblemen whose assignment was to get him drunk—and perhaps to extract information from him in the process. Herberstein, who remained sober enough to record the occasion, noted that innumerable toasts were offered, and that "the person drains the glass and holds it upside down over his head. I had no wish to drink so much, but I had no alternative."

Ivan's treatment of foreigners was only a minor aspect of his search for status—indeed, for recognition of his great achievements. Finding his palace too small, Ivan imported Italian masters to build a more imposing one. He also ordered the construction of three stone cathedrals—of the Assumption, the Archangel and the Annunciation—which still adorn the Kremlin. However, titles, ceremonies and buildings were not enough to create the air of legitimacy or "self-realization" that was required.

Accordingly, the Church, which was interested in advancing and glorifying Muscovite absolutism, made some contributions of its own. Among them was a remarkable genealogy invented for Ivan, which traced his lineage (correctly) back to the founding Varangian father, Rurik—but then went on to trace Rurik's forefathers back through 15 fictitious generations to a brother of Augustus Caesar, "proving" that Ivan was the heir of Rome not only through his marriage to Sophia, but by blood.

The most arresting tenet of the Orthodox theologians was the doctrine of the "Third Rome." It held that the first Rome had fallen into heresy, and as punishment had been overthrown by barbarians. The second Rome, Byzantium, had also become heretical—in acknowledging the supremacy of the pope, at the Council of Florence in 1438—and consequently had been overrun by the Turks. However, although "two Romes have fallen, a third stands, and a fourth there shall not be." The third Rome was Moscow, the capital of the last truly Christian nation on earth, and the residence of a czar who in his power was "similar to God in Heaven." Although this doctrine equipped the czar with ample status, it had the pernicious effect of widening still further the split between Russia and the West, and at a time when Russia was particularly in need of the culture and technology the West had to offer.

The attitude of the Church toward the monarch was not one of mere self-interest or sycophancy, although it is true that in Ivan's time the Church had secured, by grants and legacies, about 25 per cent of the cultivated land in Russia, and was not eager to lose it. The Church firmly believed in the divine establishment and right of the ruler—a conception borrowed directly from Byzantium—and several thoughtful clergymen expounded it. (The intellectual activity of this period in Russian history was confined almost entirely to the Church;

the secular world was characterized by illiteracy and violence, not by thought.) However, although a majority of churchmen believed in close cooperation between their wealthy establishment and an autocratic ruler and were willing to submit to him even in their own sphere, there were some theologians whose consciences were pricked. They could not reconcile the riches of the monasteries, and their subservience to the czar, with Christian principles as they understood them. Calling themselves "Non-Possessors," they advocated the renunciation of monastic wealth, a return to the contemplative, rigorous life, and a complete separation of church and state.

The dispute between "Possessors" and "Non-Possessors" became bitter in Ivan's day, with the "Possessors" arguing vehemently that the Church must remain wealthy in order to fulfill its charitable functions and to attract men of quality into the priesthood. Ordinarily, such a quarrel might have had small historical significance, but beneath it there lay a political issue of great importance to Ivan and the institution of czardom. Ivan had consolidated a territorial empire, but he had not been able to suppress the opposition of his boyars, who deeply resented his autocratic encroachment on their traditional rights. The boyars sided with the "Non-Possessors," hoping to deprive Ivan of a weapon (the Church) that he might use against them. Ivan was torn; he coveted the lands of the Non-Possessors, but he also wanted the divine right of kings championed by the Possessors.

The Possessors won the dispute, and the Church became even more closely identified with autocratic czardom—a circumstance that would eventually bring about the downfall of both. However, it was not Ivan's destiny to bring the boyars, or the people in general, completely under despotic rule. That grim task fell to his grandson, famous (or infamous) in history as Ivan the Terrible.

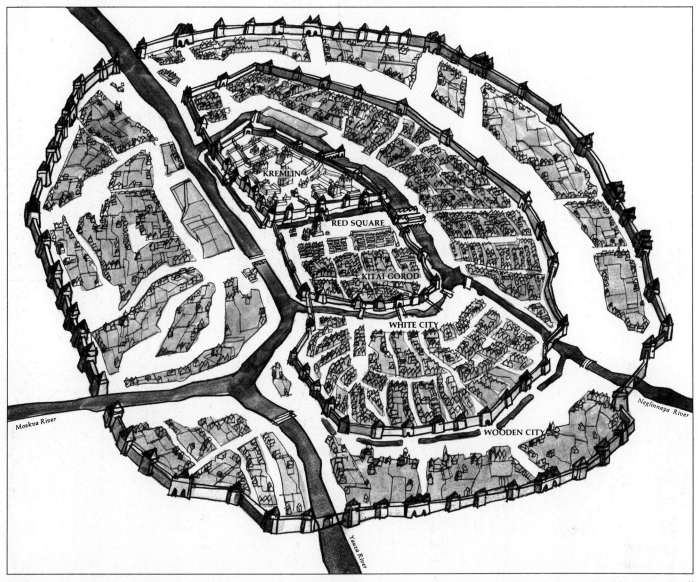

CITIES WITHIN A CITY, *medieval Moscow radiated outward from the heavily fortified Kremlin. Each ring of growth was enclosed by its own wall.*

THE FIVE LIVES OF MOSCOW

Splendor and squalor existed side by side in 17th Century Moscow, which during five centuries had grown from a crude wooden trading post on the Moskva River to a unique and vigorous capital of nearly 200,000 inhabitants. Fire, war and the pride of successive rulers constantly altered the city's face. To reconstruct the Moscow of late medieval times, Apollinari Vasnetsov, a Russian artist, spent the years from 1880 until his death in 1933 studying the city's history and archeological remains. With palette and brush he meticulously re-created the daily life and environment of Muscovites 300 years ago, from the artisans and laborers who lived in the Wooden City on the outer rim, through the merchants and boyars who inhabited the White City and Kitai Gorod *(map above)*, to the most powerful nobles, who held sway behind the Kremlin's massive wall on Red Square.

PUBLIC SAUNA BATHS, *which backed up on the Neglinnaya River, steam in the wintry air. At the right, artist Vasnetsov has shown three sweating bathers running from the steam-filled bathhouses to roll naked in the snow—a sight so common that neither the street vendor in the foreground, the passersby nor the priest at far left give them a second glance. Muscovites customarily bathed this way weekly, the wealthy using private saunas with herb-scented steam.*

THE WOODEN CITY

As medieval Moscow grew outward from its fortified Kremlin, it added rings of growth like a great tree trunk. In 1591 its outermost ring was enclosed by a wooden wall, and the broad, slush- and mud-splattered outskirt thus defined became known as the Wooden City.

It was through this outer city that a visitor to Moscow first passed, finding his way through a maze of streets lined by log houses. Here lived most of Moscow's poorer artisans and laborers—in one quarter the city's sheepskinners, in others the weavers, gardeners, coach drivers.

Fires were constantly raging through the tenement-like crush of the Wooden City, where many houses had stoves but no chimneys; the entire city is known to have burned a dozen times. Smaller fires were daily occurrences, creating a brisk business for the wood merchants outside the Pokrovsky Gate, who supplied precut logs from which a house could be built virtually overnight.

A MINSTREL TROUPE, *led by a horn-tooting dwarf and a drummer boy, draws a crowd toward a central square where its members will dance and sing and exhibit trained bears. The spike-topped wall at left guards the home of a citizen against thieves.*

THE WHITE CITY

Once he had threaded his way through the outer maze of the Wooden City, a traveler—like the man riding the white horse in the foreground of this picture—entered the older White City on his way toward Moscow's heart. This dis-

trict, named for its late-16th Century wall of white stone *(background)*, had its share of filth, wooden buildings and pungent markets, but it also had its ornate stone churches *(left)*, and grand homes *(right)*. To illustrate the great va- riety of vehicles Muscovites used, the artist set this scene during a thaw. In the middle of the street, all manner of wagons and carriages roll over the log-paved road, while off to the sides sleighs slice through the lingering snow.

BUSTLING KITAI GOROD

The first protective wall built in Moscow enclosed only the Kremlin, but as the merchants' quarter across Red Square grew more important to the city, it too was enclosed to protect it from Tartar raiders. To strengthen its first crude defenses, baskets called *kita* were filled with earth and piled against them; eventually the district came to be known as Kitai Gorod—Basket Town. By the 16th Century, Kitai Gorod had become the city's thriving center of commerce and crafts as well as the home of many wealthy boyars.

In this picture of a busy crossroads in Kitai Gorod, the artist has included a wealth of detail. Through the picture's center strides a rich merchant, staff in hand, followed by his wife, who carries a jeweled casket. Sitting with their feet in stocks at right, prisoners beg for food (the city did not feed them). The large log building that dominates the picture is an inn and tavern, as the wine pitcher over its entrance indicates. Across from the inn is the poorhouse, which also served as the local morgue. Here, under a tall bell pole, unidentified bodies are laid out in coffins while the bells toll, summoning relatives to claim them.

IN THE 16TH CENTURY, *Red Square is seen stretching the length of the Kremlin's east wall. At its far end, sheathed in scaffolding, can be seen the still-incomplete spires of St. Basil's Cathedral. While two officials watch from the steps of the city hall in the foreground, people* *afoot and on horseback hurry toward the Lobnoe Mesto in front of St. Basil's, on their way to hear a public pronouncement or perhaps to witness an execution. The bell-topped tower in the massive brick wall at right guards the Spassky Gate, the main entrance to the Kremlin.*

IN THE 17TH CENTURY *(left), a view of the square similar to that above shows its market bustling and its surrounding buildings embellished. St. Basil's is complete and its cupolas tiled. The most striking addition, however, is the tall Gothic tower atop Spassky Gate.*

SPASSKY GATE *(right), seen from the St. Basil's end of Red Square, was named for the icon of the Savior (Spas) placed on the wall above its entrance. Its bridge, spanning the Kremlin's moat, is shown lined with bookstalls where the literate of Moscow browsed.*

HISTORIC RED SQUARE

In Russian, the word for "red" also means "beautiful," and it was from that meaning that Moscow's main square derived its name. Flanked by the towers of the Kremlin, it was indeed an impressive open space, and after Ivan the Terrible built the magnificent St. Basil's Cathedral to commemorate his victories over the Tartars, it became more beautiful still. Its long, broad promenade, which separated the political and mercantile centers of the city, served Moscow much as the Forum served ancient Rome.

The political focus of Red Square was a round stone rostrum, the *Lobnoe Mesto*, which stood in the shadow of St. Basil's Cathedral. On this low stage (once proudly called the "umbilicus of the world") were played out many of the major scenes of Russian history. Here Ivan the Terrible is said to have bewailed his misrule and repented the sins of his youth. The patriarchs of the church mounted its steps to bless the people. And near it, too, countless rebels and criminals were beheaded or tortured. The daily life that swirled around the *Lobnoe Mesto*, though less dramatic, was no less colorful. From sunrise to sunset, the whole of Red Square was an open, rowdy, brawling market where all the roads from distant cities merged, and where one could buy anything from cabbages to silks.

THE GLITTERING KREMLIN

Like the painted wooden eggs that Russians give at Easter—nesting inside each other, growing more gorgeous as they grow smaller—so medieval Moscow was revealed to the traveler, step by step, until at last he came to the Kremlin itself. At its center, on an octagonal base of white stone, stood the Tower of Ivan the Great, dominating all of Moscow's other spires and battlements and epitomizing the might of the Russian czars.

In the scene at left, artist Vasnetsov has recreated the square around the base of the Ivan Tower as it looked in the 17th Century, at the height of its medieval splendor, its many-faceted rooftops embossed with snow, the more privileged of its citizens decked out in fur-trimmed caftans. While a bell in the center of the square calls people to prayer, brilliantly decorated sleighs skim over the snow-encrusted street. The small, cupola-topped structures to the right of the Ivan Tower are *chasovnyas*, private chapels belonging to influential families. At the left and rear of the picture, elaborate stairways lead to the royal palaces, from whose majestic chambers the awesome power of the czars spread to the farthest corners of the empire.

4

IVAN THE TERRIBLE

In 1547, no doubt with great trepidation, the Metropolitan of Russia placed the imperial crown on the head of Ivan IV, a 17-year-old boy who had already begun to earn the name by which history knows him—Ivan the Terrible. Intelligent and far-seeing, learned in Scripture and outwardly pious, he was at the same time as capricious a madman as has ever occupied a throne. With the name of God constantly on his lips, he ordered the death by torture of unnumbered thousands of people, and he took pleasure in devising the means and watching the agony. Yet when his victims were dead he sent lists of their names to the monasteries so that prayers could be said for their souls. At one moment brilliantly lucid, he could at the next fly into a rage and order the execution of an elephant because it would not kneel before him. Having just conducted a massacre of his own subjects, he could answer the remonstrance of a Metropolitan with a sigh of self-pity, point to the outraged churchman and say, "See how my friends and neighbors do rise against me, and conspire me evil."

Ivan the Terrible, son of Vasily III and grandson of Ivan the Great, was a child of three when his father died. For nine years, Ivan's mother, Helen, ruled the country in his name, assisted by a group of boyars. When she died (perhaps by poisoning) a struggle for control of the throne began at once among the boyars.

These aristocrats, having seen more than enough of czarist autocracy since the consolidation of Muscovy under Ivan the Great, treated his grandson with contempt verging on cruelty. They deprived him of his friends and favorite servants and lolled about on his late father's bed with their boots on. A group of them once burst into the boy's chamber at dawn and engaged in a furious argument, frightening him into a panic. In public they beat their foreheads on the ground before him, but when he was alone—according to his own account—Ivan had to go hungry and without proper clothes. Perhaps as a result of this, Ivan began very early to display the streak of sadism that marked him all his life. His childish amusement was to climb high into a Kremlin tower and throw small animals out a window; when he was old enough to ride, he would trot his horse through Moscow slashing the faces

IVAN'S CHARACTER *emerges in all its cruelty and strength in this bust reconstructed from his exhumed skull and early portraits. The face was carved in gypsum by a Soviet sculptor who was also an anthropologist.*

of his subjects with a whip. Or, as Sir Giles Fletcher noted, "If hee misliked a face or person of any man whom hee met by the way, or that looked upon him, hee would command his head to be strook off. Which was presently done, and the head cast before him."

At 13, apparently sensing the magnitude of his power for the first time, Ivan struck back at the principal boyar in the regency: he had the man seized and murdered by the Kremlin dogkeepers, and thereafter Ivan was master of Russia in fact as well as name. At 17, having delivered a startlingly adult discourse to his attendants on the comparative advantages of foreign and domestic marriage, he took as his wife a bright and beautiful young woman named Anastasia Romanov, daughter of a boyar; at 17 he arranged his own ceremony of coronation, stressing with great pomp his assertion that God had appointed him.

The state ruled by the youthful Czar, homogeneous though it was in several ways, still contained the ingredients of an explosion. Foremost among them was the bitter antagonism that had boiled for more than half a century between the autocrat in Moscow, constantly striving to make his authority absolute, and the members of the landed aristocracy, struggling to retain their traditional rights.

The aristocrats had long enjoyed the privileges of owning hereditary estates with no obligation other than the payment of taxes. They had not been required to render military or other service to a czar; many maintained private armies, dispensed justice within their own territories, and had broad independence. After the "gathering of Russia" under Ivan the Great, however, the hereditary landowners had soon found their privileges being whittled away by Moscow. No disabling laws were passed; the process was random but persistent: here the confiscation of all or part of an estate or the transfer of a boyar from his ancestral domain

to a new one in the raw hinterland; there a murder or an enforced enrollment in a monastery. Slowly the czars established the principle that ownership of land carried with it not only subservience but also the obligation of service to the state.

Apart from their drive toward absolute rule, the czars had a sound reason for coercing the boyars. Moscow had to have a large military establishment in order to defend and expand her frontiers, and it was necessary for the landed aristocracy to supply the officers and men. However, it would have been hazardous for the czars to have depended solely on the disgruntled boyars. Therefore they created a new class of landholders whose name indicates their status: service gentry.

In return for military duty, the service gentry were granted lifetime tenure on estates carved out of confiscated or newly acquired frontier land. Some of these estates were very large, capable of sustaining a family of officers and scores, or even hundreds, of peasant troops. Others were so small that they supported only one or two fighting men. But all were firmly under the control of Moscow, which could take back the land at a whim. The arrangement was ideal from the autocratic point of view—it bought the fealty of the service gentry, who could then be played off against the hereditary aristocracy.

When Ivan the Terrible came to the throne the service estate was a well-established institution, and the boyars had become at least partially resigned to the loss of their privileges and the necessity of performing duties for the czar. But many of them were still seething with anger and rebellion, and a bloody confrontation between autocrat and aristocrat was not far off.

Discontent in the upper layer of Muscovite society was matched by unrest in the lower. In order to make their estates profitable and to fulfill their obligations to Moscow, both the boyars and the service gentry needed a constant supply of peasant labor. This was assured only when the peasants were immobilized, attached firmly to the land. The traditional means of binding them in this way was through debt; a landlord would advance money to a peasant and the peasant would remain on the land until his debt had been paid. Legally, peasants could pay their debts after the fall harvest and move, taking service with another landlord who offered better terms or better land. But in fact, peasants almost never earned enough to do that; most found themselves barely able to meet the interest payments on their debts, and they thus remained, year after year, in a condition little different from bondage.

The slow, relentless process of enserfment was eroding what few liberties the peasants still had. The more adventurous of them, therefore, ran away, fleeing their debts and seeking freedom along the perimeters of the state, where they colonized lands lately wrested from the Tartars (successors of the Golden Horde) or became members of the groups of lawless frontiersmen that had come to be known as Cossacks.

Bands of Cossacks, consisting not only of peasants but also runaway slaves, criminals, Tartars and even an occasional embittered nobleman, were numerous in southern and southeastern Russia, particularly along the Don and in the Lithuanian-controlled Ukraine. Fiercely independent, electing their leaders by popular vote, the Cossacks lived largely by hunting, fishing and brigandage, and they presented a prickly problem to centralized authority; after the destruction of the *veche* town assemblies, they represented the last democratic element in Russian society. Ivan the Terrible made no attempt to subdue them—on the contrary, he was glad to accept their help against the Tartars, Poles and Lithuanians. Several Cossack leaders in fact received commissions from Moscow, becoming

auxiliaries in the Czar's army. In other regards, however, they defied him, as well as the landlords who sought to recapture runaway peasants, answering their requests with the proud boast, "There is no extradition from the Don."

The flight of peasants and small merchants from central Muscovy to the borderlands, whether because of debt, heavy taxes or the threat of military conscription, weakened the state by depopulating the towns and depriving the landholders of labor. And so long as the Cossack bands remained free, they served as a nucleus of anarchy around which insurrections could—and later did—arise.

The first years of Ivan's reign are ordinarily called his "good" period; he was not notably mad then. But it would seem that he must have been unbalanced all his life. In 1547, when the adolescent monarch had occupied the throne only a few months, he received a delegation of dignitaries from the city of Pskov who petitioned him to redress wrongs done to them by the Moscow-appointed governor. Ivan took this amiss, and began to show his displeasure by pouring boiling wine on the delegates. Then he burned off their venerable beards with a candle and ordered them to remove all their clothing and lie on the floor. What he planned to do next can only be imagined—he habitually carried a metal-pointed staff with which he skewered people who offended him, and he enjoyed searing their flesh with pans heated red-hot on a stove. At the crucial moment for the Pskovian delegates, however, a church bell chanced to fall out of a steeple nearby, and in the ensuing commotion Ivan's project slipped his mind and his victims escaped.

Soon after that incident Ivan became calm and rational, gaining a reputation as one of the ablest men who had yet ruled Moscow and, surprisingly, the most solicitous of his people. He selected a council of humanitarian advisers, including the Metropolitan, the court chaplain, and the cham-

BOAT-BORNE COSSACKS, *launched on their conquest of Siberia, are shown here under attack by tribesmen on a riverbank in an early 18th Century manuscript. They were led to safety, legend says, by a miraculous banner (left) bearing an image of Christ.*

berlain, Alexei Adashev, a man of humble origin and high integrity, and allowed himself to be guided by them. Ivan's small "Chosen Council," though it included a few boyars, was another source of irritation to the aristocracy. In their view Ivan should have relied for advice on the entire assembly of magnates, the *Duma*, which he effectively bypassed. The boyars were particularly incensed at the power given to Adashev, who, when he later fell out of the Czar's favor, was described by Ivan himself as "a man raised up from a dunghill."

Recognizing his country's need for technical skills, Ivan sent to Europe for scholars and engineers. In 1550 he convened the first *Zemsky Sobor*—an "assembly of the land"—in which the clergy, the hereditary aristocracy, the service gentry and probably even the merchants were represented. The Zemsky Sobor was by no means a true parliament; its members were appointed, not elected, and their function was not to debate the Czar's proposals but simply to approve them. Still Ivan listened carefully to the grievances that were presented and took steps to remedy the causes of some of them. In a remarkable speech he asked forgiveness for past injustices, explaining that as an orphan he had learned evil ways from the boyars who surrounded him, and promising thenceforth to be a more admirable ruler. "How I have sinned, and how many punishments has God sent against you! And I did not repent, and I have myself persecuted poor Christians with every violence."

Following the Zemsky Sobor, Ivan ordered the remodeling and liberalization of the law code, instructed Adashev to find means of appointing better judges, and established a permanent bureau to receive petitions. He also reformed the system of provincial government—if the various districts would guarantee payments to Moscow every year, they could elect their own tax collectors and other officials, and would no longer have to endure the rapacity of czarist appointees. Moreover, the provinces could choose their own magistrates to suppress crime, which had been increasing under the appointed governors.

After this auspicious beginning in domestic affairs Ivan turned to the frontiers in the east and southeast. His predecessors had broken the Mongol yoke, but separate khanates remained strong and menacing. Now Ivan launched a retaliatory drive—the counterstroke of long-suffering Orthodoxy against the infidels, of the forest against the steppe—and at the head of 100,000 troops supported by scores of cannon, he battered his way into the khanate of Kazan. In 1552 he took its great fortress, situated near the junction of the Volga and Kama Rivers, and opened the way for the long Russian march into Asia. Four years later, under Russian pressure and weakened by internal strife, the khanate of Astrakhan surrendered to Ivan. The Russian empire thus came to include the entire course of the Volga south to the Caspian Sea.

Ivan's victories over the Tartars greatly endeared

him to the Russian people; even his later domestic atrocities, which were directed mainly against the wealthy, failed to tarnish his memory. Ivan's epithet, "The Terrible," is a translation of a Russian word that means "awesome," not "awful." Russians remember Ivan as having been awesome to the enemies of the people, not to the people themselves.

After the fall of Kazan and Astrakhan only the khanate of the Crimea remained to be conquered in the south. Ivan's advisers urged him to make an assault on it but he rejected the idea; the Crimea was too well fortified, and he feared that an attack on it might provoke the Turks. In any case he had turned his eyes toward Europe.

In 1554 the English explorer Richard Chancellor, searching for a northern trade route to the Orient, had sailed into the White Sea and made a landfall near the mouth of the northern Dvina. He journeyed south to Moscow and "discovered" Russia, a nation of which his countrymen knew almost nothing: as late as Shakespeare's time, Englishmen believed that cannibalism was common in Russia and that the country was full of fantastic creatures such as the "vegetable lamb," which had the appearance of a small sheep but was green and attached to a stalk that grew out of the ground.

Chancellor quickly recognized the advantages of a commercial treaty and found Ivan more than willing to make one. The Czar soon developed a strong partiality for the English which influenced his policies for many years. He engaged in a long correspondence with Elizabeth I, and apparently entertained the idea of proposing marriage. When it appeared that the Virgin Queen was not inclined to give herself to someone called Ivan the Terrible, he negotiated for the hand of an English noblewoman. Nothing came of that, but commercial relations burgeoned. (At one time ropes and cables from Russia, which were considered to be the best in the world, were used on most of the ships in the English navy.)

The ties with England reinforced Ivan's desire to draw closer to the West and he saw but one way to do it: to cut his way though to the Baltic in order to obtain a warm-water port and a "window" through which exchanges might pass. The White Sea ports were too often blocked by ice to carry the volume of commerce he envisioned. However, his way to the Baltic was barred by the German Knights of the Sword, who occupied the coastal region between Sweden and Poland then known as Livonia. In 1558 Ivan attacked Livonia and at first he met with considerable success. But soon both Poland and Sweden entered the war and it settled into a 25-year bloodletting that ended in Russian defeat.

Ivan's effort and intent in this war are of historical consequence. Here, in the mid-16th Century, Russia made her first great attempt to establish and develop commercial and cultural relations with the West—and was sealed off by an "Iron Curtain," which was interposed by bordering states and which was fully as impenetrable as the one on her side that was to be decried by Winston Churchill four centuries later. Sweden and Poland wished to keep Russia in isolation and ignorance, and succeeded in doing so. They repeatedly blocked the passage of scholars and technicians whom Ivan invited from the West. When Ivan appealed to Queen Elizabeth for help, King Sigismund Augustus of Poland made the matter quite plain. He implored her to refuse Ivan, adding, "Up to now we could conquer him only because he was a stranger to education and did not know the arts."

While the brutal Livonian war dragged on, Ivan slipped into the "bad" period of his life. His fear and suspicion of the boyars, amply justified in some cases, slowly became paranoiac. At 23 he had suffered a serious illness, and in the belief that he was dying had called on the boyars to swear allegiance to his infant son. The boyars were reluctant, and when Ivan recovered he was more vindictive than ever.

In 1560, when Ivan was 30, his wife Anastasia, whom he deeply loved and who had exercised a warm and gentling influence on him, died after a lingering illness, and Ivan suffered a severe emotional collapse. Convinced that the boyars had poisoned her, he lashed out at his closest aides, conducting a bloody purge in which not only boyars but their families and servants were murdered, or imprisoned and tortured. Two princely boyars were executed without trial, merely for lodging a mild protest, and others fled to Lithuania, strengthening Ivan's conviction that the aristocracy did in fact "conspire me evil."

In 1564 Ivan began a hegira so strange and sudden that it staggered the people of Moscow. A great train of sledges appeared outside the Kremlin and were loaded with his treasures (an English observer noted that he had enough gold plates to serve 1,700 people). Carrying the core of retainers who still enjoyed his trust, the train of sledges was dragged 60 miles northeast to the small town of Aleksandrov, where Ivan immured himself. For a month nothing was heard from him, and then two letters were delivered to the Metropolitan. In one, Ivan denounced both the boyars and the clergy —his wrath fell on the Church not only because its spokesmen had dared to quarrel with him, but for a practical reason. He had constant need of new land on which to establish estates for his service gentry, yet the Church had expanded its holdings to include almost one third of the most productive territory in central Russia. The Holy Trinity-St. Sergius Monastery north of Moscow alone had 100,000 workers on its property. In the second letter Ivan assured the common people of Moscow of his affection.

Panic-stricken, both the boyars and the ordinary citizens implored Ivan to return as czar. However mad he may have been, he was the victor over the Tartars along the Volga and the linchpin of government, and without him there could be only anarchy. Relenting, Ivan came back to Moscow. He was grievously changed in physical appearance. Apparently he had undergone a racking emotional crisis: his once-bright gray eyes were glazed and dull, and only wisps remained of his hair and beard. He would resume his duties, he said, on two conditions: he must be given the right to judge "traitors" as he alone defined them, and to punish them as he saw fit; and he must be allowed to establish an *oprichnina*.

The oprichnina, the name of which was derived from the Russian for "apart" or "beside," was to be in effect a state within a state. To govern it, and to keep the rest of the country in line, Ivan intended to create a new elite (oprichniks) owing its position and its loyalty to him alone. To achieve this Ivan wanted to create a fantastic gerrymander; the oprichnina was to comprise not only the territories he considered loyal or vital to him, but huge boyar domains that he intended to confiscate and redistribute. The remainder of the country, the *zemshchina*, was to exist under the status quo. As it finally developed, the oprichnina came to include almost half of Russia and was beyond geographical description. It included certain districts, even specific blocks, within Moscow, but not others; some boyar estates were inside it, others outside; even individuals were singled out—English traders, for example, were classified as oprichniks while many Russian merchants were not.

As what some historians believe to be an ironic gesture, Ivan officially reduced his own title to "Prince of Moscow," and in the zemshchina he set up a puppet "Czar of all Russia," a newly converted and doubtless bewildered Tartar named

Semyon Bukbulatovich, to whom he pretended to render homage.

Whatever Ivan's secondary purposes may have been in establishing the oprichnina, his prime one was to quash rebellion, or the possibility of it, within the aristocracy. Even though several of the oprichniks were themselves boyars, the majority were service gentry and others—Tartars, Germans, Lithuanians, Cossacks—of relatively modest origin: it was the pitting of class against class. The oprichniks were, in effect, a dread secret police, ultimately numbering in the thousands—ferocious men dressed in black, riding black horses, who stormed through the country with brooms and dogs' heads hanging from their saddles. The dogs' heads were meant to symbolize their duty of worrying the enemies of the Czar, the brooms their intent to sweep treason from the land.

The oprichniks raged in Russia for approximately eight years, during which so many people were dispossessed or killed that Ivan himself lost all track, remarking that "God knows their names." The unfortunate boyars offered no resistance—divided among themselves, united only in the desire to keep their hereditary lands and privileges, they submitted to torture and death with surprising meekness. Not only individuals but entire cities felt Ivan's wrath. Suspecting that Novgorod had entered into negotiations with Lithuania, he conducted a six-weeks' slaughter in which numberless citizens were mutilated and roasted to death in the public square, while others were thrown into the river where oprichniks in boats pushed them under the ice to drown.

Forsaking Moscow, Ivan established headquarters in a fortified palace at Aleksandrov, and while his forces of terror swept the land, he ruled a weird parody of a monastery. His oprichniks were "monks" and he was the "abbot." After prostrating himself before an altar with such vehemence that his forehead would be bloody and covered with bruises, he would rise and read homilies on the Christian virtues to his drunken retainers, fresh from torturing and raping victims in the cellars. Frequently he would act as master of the rituals in which, with sharp and hissing-hot pincers, ribs were torn out of men's chests. Some of his tortures, as reported by foreigners such as the Englishman Jerome Horsey, cannot even be mentioned without the alterations here made in the original text: "Prince Boris Telupa, discovered to be a 'traitor' against the Emperor, was drawn upon a long sharp-made stake, which entered the lower part of his body and came out of his neck; upon which he languished a horrible pain for 15 hours alive, and spoke to his mother, the duchess, brought to behold that woeful sight. And she, a good matronly woman, was then given to 100 gunners, who defiled her to death, and the Emperor's hungry hounds devoured her flesh and bones."

When Ivan dissolved the oprichnina, the hereditary aristocracy, as a political force, was dead. However, many of the leading aristocrats remained alive, and in time their descendants would rise again to struggle with Ivan's successors. As his near-contemporary, Machiavelli, might have pointed out, Ivan made the error of destroying individual aristocrats rather than wiping out the entire class, and his methods lacked the finesse of the Tudors in England who, beset with similar problems, brought the aristocrats to heel with less bloodshed and more lasting effect through discreet banishments, mysterious murders and behind-the-scenes intrigue.

Throughout Ivan's reign, while boyars and oprichniks came and went, the Russian people continued to extend their country's boundaries. None of this territorial expansion was accomplished by czarist plan or order. It was the result of a spontaneous movement of the people, who, like their

American counterparts, were seeking either wealth or freedom in an unexploited land. But, unlike Americans, who had a straight frontier along the Atlantic seaboard and could proceed only toward the setting sun, the Russians had a circular frontier, radiating from Moscow. They could make but little progress against Poland and Sweden in the west, but the roads north, east and south were open to them.

Colonial expansion was particularly rapid in the northeast, where the lure of gold and furs attracted many hardy men. Among these was a Cossack, Ermak Timofeevich, who, with a band of fewer than 1,000 men armed with superior weapons—guns against bows and lances—defeated the Khan of Sibir east of the Urals and offered his conquest to Ivan. The Czar accepted the new territory and sent reinforcements.

In a remarkably short time, far more rapidly than Americans settled the west, Russians pushed on to the Pacific, more than doubling the size of their empire in less than 70 years. In 1630 they reached Yakutsk on the great Lena River, and in 1647 stood on the shores of the Sea of Okhotsk. There they encountered the power of the Manchu Chinese, who also possessed firearms, and an uneasy truce was established along the line of the Stanovoy Mountains, preventing further Russian movement into Manchuria to the south for two centuries.

On the southern and southeastern flanks of Muscovy other gains were made by Cossacks and colonists, but the gains were smaller and made at greater cost. Remnants of Tartar tribes and the massed power of the still unconquered khanate of the Crimea presented a formidable threat. In Ivan's time the steppe defenses were strengthened by the establishment of fortified towns and hamlets, manned by the newly created service gentry; there were Cossack watch posts and earthworks, and a remarkable movable palisade, like a collapsible picket fence, some 70 miles in length and loopholed for guns.

Still the Crimean Tartars broke through. In 1571—guided, it was said, by dissident boyars who knew the unguarded paths—they reached Moscow and wreaked unbelievable slaughter, burning the city and killing at least 100,000 people (a resident Englishman put the figure at 800,000). The Moscow River was so choked with bodies that its course was diverted, and the water was crimson for miles downstream. Retreating, the Tartars carried off hundreds of people into slavery—the prime captives were young girls, who were carried in baskets slung from the Tartars' saddles. But even in chains the Russians were difficult to handle—persistent and ingenious in escape. The slave merchants, crying their wares in Byzantium, made a point of saying that the captives were from "the kingdom"—i.e., Lithuania—and therefore more docile than those from Russia.

Ivan the Terrible died in 1584; in his last days he wandered howling through his palace, his cries audible to those outside. Forsaking even the pretense of Christianity, he sought comfort in the prophecies of witches and magicians brought to Moscow from the far north, where paganism still flourished. Every day he would command his attendants to carry him in a chair into his treasury. There he would pluck rich jewels from their coffers and hold them against his skin; he fancied that the jewels changed color, indicating that he was "poisoned with disease."

On the day of his death Ivan appeared to rally; he sang merry songs and called for his chessboard, but before he could begin his game he suddenly toppled backward and died. So violent had been his reign, and so prodigious the force of his twisted personality, that it is difficult to credit his true age: he was only 54.

AWAITING THE SERVICE, *worshipers assemble reverently in the ancient, dimly lit cathedral of the Monastery of the Holy Trinity near Moscow.*

A LUMINOUS LITURGY

Russia's love of sacred pageantry was expressed in the sumptuous services of the Orthodox Church, whose holy days, celebrated by every Russian, accounted for almost one third of the days of the year. Scores of monasteries trained priests to perform the elaborate liturgy; workshops operated by church and state produced a never-ending array of jeweled icons, silk banners, brocaded vestments and gold chalices; and even small villages boasted magnificent male choirs.

Nowhere was the richness of Orthodoxy more spectacularly displayed than at the vast Monastery of the Holy Trinity, now the city of Zagorsk. This community, some 40 miles outside Moscow, became Russia's wealthiest and most famous monastery, and was for centuries a center of sacred studies. Even today it continues to hold services that faithfully preserve the dazzling traditions of the past.

PIOUS PATRIARCHS IN ROYAL ROBES

As Christianity itself originally came from Byzantium to Russia, so a large part of the Russian Orthodox liturgy was borrowed from the court ceremony of Byzantine emperors, who had been regarded by their subjects as the representatives of Christ on earth.

Before the service itself began, the presiding bishop or patriarch donned majestic robes in full view of the congregation, a ritual that closely resembled the emperor's elaborate procedures for dressing. The vestments themselves were also patterned after Byzantine regalia. The bishops' miters were copies of the imperial crown and their robes were made of regal materials.

The fabrics and jewels of the vestments reflected the best of what was available both at home and abroad: Italian velvets and brocades, silk woven in Constantinople and embroidered with gold and silver threads in Russia, emeralds from the Ural Mountains, turquoises from Persia, rubies from the Orient, pearls from the Crimea and the Persian Gulf. Once he was adorned in such royal raiment, a bishop was ready to officiate in the church, which the Russians called "the palace of God."

A BISHOP'S VESTMENTS *include a 12th Century jeweled cameo of the Crucifixion (top) and a rich caftan or robe embroidered with pearls. The caftan was worn by Nikon, the reformist who was a 17th Century Patriarch of Muscovy.*

SITTING IN STATE, *a 20th Century Patriarch of*

Moscow, who wears around his shoulders an omophorion, or bishop's stole, is flanked by two deacons; next to them, wearing miters, are two bishops.

A GLORIOUS PROCESSION

After the Patriarch was dressed, he commenced the service, which might last three or four hours. At one point, he led a grand procession, in which the Book of the Gospels was carried from the altar, through the nave and back to the altar

RAISING THE GOSPELS *(left), a deacon halts the procession through the church. To the right of the patriarch is a stylized fan, an ancient Byzantine symbol of imperial rank.*

A PAINTED CRUCIFIX, *made in Novgorod about 1500, was borne in sacred processions. Above Christ are the Saints Michael and Gabriel; flanking Him are the Virgin and St. John.*

again. As he made his slow progress about the church, a male choir sang sonorous hymns and a deacon swung a censer that poured forth clouds of perfumed smoke. The members of the congregation stood throughout the service—but they seldom stood still. On witnessing a rural service, one French observer remarked, "The peasant prays with all his limbs . . . crossing himself, raising at the same time his head and his right hand, then bending in two between every sign of the Cross."

A GOLD GOSPEL COVER, *created in the Kremlin workshops in 1678, is embossed with enameled decorations. The Gospel writers—Matthew, Mark, Luke and John—are shown at the corners. The center medallion, seen in the detail below, depicts Christ seated between Mary and St. John.*

RICH SETTINGS
FOR HOLY WORDS

Soon after the grand procession came the part of the service the people most loved to hear: the reading of the Gospels. So deep was the Russians' respect for the Scriptures that czars spent fortunes having the sacred books bound; one covering of jewel-studded gold, commissioned in the late 17th Century, weighed 57 pounds and represented months of effort by the nation's most highly skilled craftsmen.

Few Russians other than priests could read the Gospels for themselves, and fewer still read secular works. Monasteries ran schools for laymen, but they were remote and poorly attended, and the few students who learned to read usually restricted themselves to religious works, chiefly the New Testament and the lives of saints. The Book of Psalms was the beginning reader's first primer and a common devotional manual for everyone. Secular books of any sort were feared and hated; and imported ones were hated most of all; the Russians' religious zeal, bound up with their proud nationalism, led them to a profound mistrust of all foreign writers.

So strong was the Russians' dislike of secular literature that when they wanted to imply that a man had lost his senses, they would say: "He has gone into books."

CHANTING VERSES, *a bearded reader faces the iconostasis, or altar screen, and sings from the Gospels as two acolytes stand in attendance.*

HOLY COMMUNION AND A FINAL BLESSING

The climax of the service was the Eucharist, the ceremony in which the priests entered the sanctuary to bless the bread and wine—i.e., Christ's body and blood. Following this they emerged to offer Holy Communion to the congregation.

Russians believed that many miracles were connected with the Eucharist. Saint Sergius, the 14th Century founder of the Holy Trinity Monastery, insisted upon baking the holy bread with his own hands, and legend recounts that an angel in shining raiment often helped him sanctify it. The first time Saint Sergius received the Eucharist as a boy, it is said, he was immediately granted by God the ability to read and understand the Holy Scriptures.

AN ENAMELED CHALICE (above), used for sacramental wine, is adorned with jewels and a picture of Christ.

CELEBRATING THE EUCHARIST (left), priests bless the wine and bread as incense rises around the altar table.

A LAST BENEDICTION (right) is conferred by the presiding patriarch on the congregation as it leaves.

5

AN ADAMANT FAITH

In the unique style of Russian Christianity lies one of the keys—perhaps the major one—to an understanding of the people and their history.

From their earliest pagan days to the present, Russians have been deeply moved by beauty in all its forms: in nature, in the innocence of children, in the courage of the old, in love, music and art. Beauty stirs in the Russian heart a feeling called *umilenie*, which falls just short of tears; in it tenderness, sadness and exaltation are combined. A man incapable of responding to beauty with *umilenie* is, to the Russian mind, dead to the world.

In the late 10th Century, according to the half-legendary account in the *Primary Chronicle*, the emissaries of Grand Prince Vladimir of Kiev returned from Byzantium with the advice that he adopt the Eastern Orthodox faith. It is unlikely that the emissaries understood the Greek words of the service they attended in the cathedral of Hagia Sofia, or had any real grasp of its religious meaning. What stirred and attracted them was the religion's beauty, the chants and the robes of the clergy, the icons, incense and architecture. "For on earth there is no such splendor or such beauty and we are at a loss to describe it."

Although the account may not be correct in fact, it rings true in spirit. Vladimir's emissaries were filled with *umilenie*, overwhelmed by what they saw, heard and felt—rather than by theological or philosophical ideas. In later centuries the Russians would fall into closely reasoned religious debates, but an outstanding characteristic of their faith has always been its deeply emotional quality.

The upper classes of Kievan society accepted Orthodoxy with wholehearted enthusiasm. From Byzantium they adopted the Orthodox service almost intact, delighting in its combination of earthly and spiritual beauty. In the Eastern service such central events as the birth, death and resurrection of Christ are commemorated with a dramatic power unknown in the West. The church itself is not regarded merely as a nominal "House of God," but as His actual dwelling place. There are no musical instruments; all the music is vocal. There are no chairs; the worshipers all stand, sometimes for several hours, both in reverence and as a faint reminder of the agony of Christ on the Cross.

Russians also accepted without question the use of icons: two-dimensional portraits of Christ, the Holy Family and the saints. To the Western mind, icons have sometimes appeared irreconcilable with the commandment against the making of graven images, but to Byzantines or Russians this is not at all the case. Icons are never worshiped, but only venerated—actual worship passes through the icons and arises to God.

Despite their acceptance of many Byzantine elements, the newly converted Russians soon began to interpret Christianity in their own way: they tended to stress Christ's compassion, rather than emphasize His divinity as the Byzantines did.

Thus the core of Russian belief became kenotic; i.e., it stressed the emulation of Christ, in His poverty, meekness and love, as the path to salvation. Soon after the conversion there emerged in Russia the first of her great monastic leaders, St. Theodosius, whose life typifies one aspect of the kenotic ideal. A young man of nobility and wealth, he rejected his privileges, put on the "uncouth garb" of a peasant and became a laborer. In time he found his way into the Kievan Monastery of the Caves, where he was made abbot, and for many years he directed the monastery in its work of caring for the poor. Physically powerful, he voluntarily assumed the heavy tasks of monks who were too weak or weary to perform them. In the words of a biography written about the beginning of the 12th Century, "He was animated by real humility and great gentleness; in everything he imitated Christ, our true God, Who said: 'He that will be first among you shall be your servant.' Contemplating Christ's humility, he humbled himself, putting himself in the lowest place as an example to others."

According to his biographer, Theodosius and the monks were constantly engaged in fighting evil spirits. "One evening, when our father was rest-ing, a great tumult arose in the caves, caused by a horde of demons. It sounded as if some of them were driving around in a carriage, while others played on tambourines and flutes; all together they made a hubbub that shook the caves to their very foundations. But Father Theodosius remained untroubled and unafraid. He arose, made the sign of the cross and began to chant the psalms of David, and at once the noise subsided."

These demons were very real to the early Christians of Kiev, who regarded them as old pagan gods, furious at the conversion, who refused to die. (In fact, they did not die easily. For centuries many Russians practiced dvoeverie, or double faith, mingling Christianity and heathenism.)

In summarizing Theodosius' character, the biographer spoke not only of his power over demons, his deliberate poverty and tireless labor, but also of his Christlike willingness to endure abuse.

St. Theodosius, exemplary though he was of the kenotic ideal, was not the first Russian to be canonized. That honor fell to two young princes, Boris and Gleb, who were caught up in the fratricidal war that followed the death of their father, Vladimir. Their story illustrates another, more fatalistic side of kenoticism.

According to the old accounts, Prince Boris, returning from an expedition against the Pechenegs, received word of his father's death and was also told that his older brother, Svyatopolk, intended to kill him to remove him as a possible rival for the throne. Meditating on his perils, Boris concluded that he owed obedience to Svyatopolk regardless of his brother's intentions, and, more important, that "The Lord resists the proud, and gives His grace to the humble. If he sheds my blood, I shall be a martyr to my Lord."

So Boris calmly awaited his death; as he was struck down his final words were, "Thou knowest, my Lord, that I do not resist, do not object."

PROSTRATE GUARDSMEN *bow in reverence as the annual Palm Sunday procession passes into the Kremlin from Moscow's Red Square. After a service at St. Basil's Church, barely visible at left, the Czar gave an address from the small amphitheater in the foreground. Then the procession formed and wound into the Czar's palace through the Spassky Gate. At the rear, the Czar on foot led the Patriarch on horseback, re-enacting Christ's entry into Jerusalem. Preceding them, a dead tree hung with fresh fruit was dragged on a sled on which boys stood singing hymns.*

Gleb, who was scarcely more than a boy, was also marked for death by Svyatopolk. However, he lacked the lofty resignation of Boris and despairingly pleaded for his life. "Don't do me any harm, my dear brethren, please don't. I did you no evil . . . Do not reap me from my immature life, do not reap the unripe ear. Do not cut down the vineshoot which is not yet grown up." But at the last, Gleb accepted his fate, recognizing that in his death he was following Christ.

Another characteristic of Russian spirituality is an intense love of nature. All Christians recognize the universe as the handiwork of God, but Kievan Russians saw in nature particular evidence of God's love. The great *Testament* of Vladimir Monomakh illustrates the lofty ethical standards that Christianity inculcated in many—though certainly not all—Russian leaders. It also suggests the Russian sense of the religious values of nature:

"Who would not praise, not glorify Thy might and Thy great wonders and beauties found in this world—how the sky is ordered; how the sun, moon and stars, darkness and light, and the earth laid upon waters, Oh Lord, by Thy providence; various animals, and birds and fishes adorned by Thy providence, Oh Lord! . . . Let us also wonder how the birds of the skies go from their paradise, fall into our hands but stay not in one country but go, strong and weak alike, over all countries, by order of God, to all forests and fields."

In an anonymous work of the Kievan period, *The Sermon of the Celestial Powers*, a writer envisioned the rebirth of the world after the Last Judgment, and took such delight in describing the beauties of nature that he omitted mention of the happy state of men. "Afterward, the earth will be new . . . as it was in the beginning, and whiter than snow; it will be changed by the order of God, and will be like gold; there will grow upon it various grasses and flowers, never fading, because spiritual; and trees will come forth, not similar to those visible now; their height, beauty and splendor the lips of men are unable to express, because they are spiritual." The great Russian-American scholar of religion, G. P. Fedotov, found this vision of the transfigured earth "supremely Russian."

The Kievan peasants were the slowest to accept Christianity. The self-imposed poverty and humility of St. Theodosius and the voluntary suffering of Boris and Gleb were comprehensible only to the upper class. When the link with Byzantium was all but broken by the Mongol conquest, even the members of that class were so demoralized that they lost sight of the golden ideals. The Church itself, although it mediated between the Russians and their conquerors, was ruinously disorganized.

However, it was the Church that began to lead the way toward national revival. Seeking solitude and peace in which they could practice their humble Christianity, scores of monks established themselves in the wilderness north and northeast of Moscow. Many at first were hermits, but soon other religious men clustered around them. Hermitages became monasteries; and monasteries, grown large, sent missionaries still deeper into the forests. Between 1340 and 1500 literally hundreds of religious centers sprang up in the dark north, sparks of light and outposts of colonization.

Foremost among the hermit monks were Sergius of Radonezh, who founded the Holy Trinity Monastery north of Moscow and became the patron saint of Muscovite Russia. Like Theodosius, Sergius was a kenotic, although he placed considerably more value on learning than his predecessor had, and appears to have been one of the most cultured Russians of his century—he died in 1392. Sergius was also the first of the native saints to have mystical experiences, thus adding a new depth to Russian spirituality: in his prayers he is said to have seen and conversed with the Virgin, and when he stretched out his hands to bless one of his disciples, unearthly light flickered at his fingertips.

Sergius' character, wisdom and mysticism won him an enormous reputation; as a result he became heavily involved in the worldly affairs of Moscow. The Muscovite princes were then engaged in their "gathering" of Russia, and Sergius was called upon to bless their troops before the battle of Kulikovo, to intervene in their disputes, and generally to lend his ecclesiastical support to their cause. From this aspect of his life's work—social and political—stemmed one of the two divergent paths Russian monasticism was to take: support of the Czar, and practical, everyday involvement in secular life. From the other aspect of Sergius's work—the kenotic and mystical—the second path: independence of the czars, deep spirituality and renunciation of worldly power and wealth. The two tendencies, each with great impact on Russian religious life, were destined to cause repeated clashes in the centuries that followed.

After the fall of Byzantium in 1453 and the breaking of formal Mongol domination in 1480, church and state worked together to make Russia the great bastion of Orthodoxy. Theologians advanced the doctrine of Moscow as "the third Rome" and revived the Byzantine theory that the Czar had absolute authority in secular affairs and the Patriarch had similar powers in churchly matters. Each supplemented the other, and together they headed a perfect Christian state. However, this balance was easily upset and the trend in Muscovy was toward Caesaropapism, in which the

Czar was supreme in both church and state. The Czar assumed the right to appoint the Metropolitan and to depose him at will—in 1521, when the Metropolitan protested against the brutality of Vasily III, he was exiled and replaced by a more "sensible" man. In 1568, for making a similar protestation, Metropolitan Philip was imprisoned and strangled by order of Ivan the Terrible.

Such grim affairs were not commonplace—some of the czars allowed themselves to be dominated by leaders of the Church—but the threat was always present. The Church thus surrendered part of its authority, and in return accepted the protection of the Czar, who was committed to defend it against its enemies—heretics and Catholics—and to leave inviolate the rich lands under monastic control.

Although the advancement of the Czar's protection might well have been bitterly resisted by all the clergy, there were many who welcomed it. Among them was the Abbot Joseph of Volokolamsk, who followed the worldly, social-national form of monasticism that constituted half of the heritage of St. Sergius. Joseph, though saintly and admirable in his personal life, was an uncompromising man who placed strong emphasis on the outward forms of religion—the precise performance of rituals and liturgical prayers—and believed in "obedience without reasoning." Ruthless in his attitude toward heretics, he felt that the police powers of the Czar should be employed harshly against all who deviated from old-established ritual or dogma, and he was well satisfied with the order of Vasily III: "Cut off the tongues of some heretics, and deliver the others to fire!"

In opposition to Joseph stood Nilus Sorsky, a monk from beyond the Volga, in whom shone forth the second half of St. Sergius' legacy, the mystical and the gentle. Nilus, backed by many holy men along the frontiers, argued that the Czar had no power in spiritual affairs, that heretics should be converted not by torture but by persuasion and prayer, and that true Christianity was less a matter of ritualism than of humility and devotion. The struggle between the followers of Nilus and Joseph—the poor, evangelical frontier religion and the wealthy, ritualistic urban religion—disrupted the Church for two generations in 16th Century Russia. Victory at last was won by the Josephites, who continued to support the Czar while the disciples of Nilus fled deeper into the forest. However, the fundamental questions of ritualism and church-state relations were only temporarily put aside; in time they would rise again to provoke a schism from which the Church would never recover.

Victory of the Josephites was made total early in the reign of Ivan the Terrible, who convened a series of ecclesiastical councils in which the rituals and customs of the Church were laid down as immutable law. Among the important points were these: the sign of the cross must be made with two fingers, not one or three; Church processions must move with, not against, the sun; to shave the beard is a gross sin; and the Alleluia must be repeated only twice in the liturgy. The councils also took steps to aggrandize the Russian Church in the Orthodox world as a whole. One step toward this, they felt, was the establishment of a large roster of native saints—Russia had only a few, and the sainthood of some of them, including the beloved Boris and Gleb, had not been recognized by Byzantium. Accordingly, in three years no fewer than 37 new saints, most of them princes, were added to the roll—more than had been canonized in all the centuries since the conversion.

There remained another point of pride to be assuaged. The various Eastern Churches, unlike the Roman, were united in faith but not under a single head. There were patriarchs in Byzantium, Antioch, Alexandria and Jerusalem—but Russia had only a Metropolitan, nominally subordinate to Byzantium. Therefore in 1589, a few years after Ivan's death, Moscow elevated the Metropolitan, Job, to the rank of patriarch, with the concurrence of the other Churches. In seniority he was last, but in Russian eyes, and as a practical matter, since most of the others were under Turkish domination, his see was unquestionably the most important.

With its Patriarch and its saints and its multitude of churches—to foreigners it seemed that the whole land was alive with the sound of bells—Russian Orthodoxy had a grand façade. Behind it, however, the view was not altogether inspiring. Saints Theodosius, Sergius, Joseph and Nilus were all well-educated men, by the standards of their time and place, and the Church had produced a few scholars of true brilliance. St. Stephen of Perm, a 14th Century contemporary of St. Sergius, and the outstanding missionary in Russian Church history, took as his assignment the conversion of the Zyrian tribes in the far north near the White Sea. In 13 years of study he mastered their extremely difficult dialects and runes, learned Greek as well as Church Slavonic, and became an icon painter in the bargain. But such men were rare in the higher levels of the Church, and not found at all in the lower.

The problem was not wholly a Churchly one—illiteracy was almost universal. However, the lack of education among the clergy led Church leaders to confuse the trappings of religion with its substance. For this reason the items formally promulgated by the ecclesiastical councils under Ivan the Terrible were not trivial, as they may seem to the modern, Western mind; they were of the utmost importance. If a man did not use two fingers in making the sign of the cross, he was guilty not of a mere inadvertence but of a dreadful sin. The slightest deviation from the established wording of a religious text could provoke a furious dispute.

The decline in the intellectual life of the Church was matched by a decline in the observance of Church law: drunkenness among the clergy, and an unwillingness to observe fasts, were commonplace. Early in the 17th Century, therefore, the leading clergy instituted a threefold program of reform: moral, administrative and intellectual, the latter involving the correction of religious texts in the hope of assuring uniformity and accuracy. The moral, spiritual reform was successful, at least among the upper classes, to a point that bordered on the absurd. The Czar and his court attended services that lasted seven hours—the Patriarch of Antioch, Macarius, visiting Russia in 1654-1656, was appalled: "Now what shall we say," he wrote, "of these duties, severe enough to turn children's hair grey, so strictly observed by the Emperor, Patriarch, grandees, princesses, and ladies, standing upright on their legs from morning to evening?"

The correction of religious books, with accompanying changes in the rituals, was at first approached with great caution. The work was done primarily by scholars from a university in Kiev, who had come to Moscow and been installed in the government printing house. No doubt *any* alterations in texts and rituals would have been opposed, but changes suggested by Kievans were particularly suspect. Kiev had long been under the domination of Catholic Poland, and in Muscovite eyes the Kievan scholars had been infected with detestable Catholic, Western ideas. However, the scholars received the support of the Russian Patriarch, Nikon, and in 1652 there began a fatal quarrel that led to the schism and disruption of the Church.

Nikon, perhaps the most brilliant man who ever headed the Russian Church, was also the most overweening and dictatorial. In his view, the Church had deviated from the original ritualism inherited from Byzantium, and must return to the "old" Greek customs. In fact he decreed that every detail of contemporary Greek practice should be adopted by the Russians. With the support of the pious and somewhat weak-willed Czar Alexis, Nikon ordained a number of ritualistic changes, the most controversial of which was the making of the sign of the cross with three fingers, not two. To many Russians this constituted not simply an alteration in symbolism, but a basic change in faith. Further, the three-fingered sign was not in fact an old Greek usage; it was of fairly recent origin.

Nikon pushed through his changes with implacable zeal, and the Czar's police rigorously backed him. In consequence, a large segment of the Russian clergy, calling themselves "Old Believers," rebelled against both Patriarch and Czar. Why, they asked, should "Holy Russia," the third and final Rome, change its ancient ways? Were not the Kievan book revisers, who insisted on spelling the name of the Savior "Iesus" instead of "Isus," the true heretics? Was not Byzantium, under Turkish rule, weak in faith?

The great leader of the Old Believers was the Archpriest Avvakum, to whom established ritualism and puritanism were all-important. Almost incredibly devout, Avvakum followed the custom, each night before going to sleep, of saying 600 prayers to Jesus and 100 to Mary. These prayers were accompanied by 300 prostrations, in each of which he would touch his forehead to the ground and rise again to his feet.

Avvakum, who had earlier collaborated with Nikon in the moral reform of the Church, at first appealed to the Patriarch and the Czar in the name of reason. Unheeded, he then endured 29 years of harassment, much of it in exile in Siberia. Toward the end of his life he wrote a remarkable autobiography, the finest Russian literary work of the 17th Century, in which he documented his sufferings. In one section he noted: "To my village came dancing bears with tambourines and lutes, and I, miserable sinner, full of zeal for Christ, drove them out. I broke the tambourines and lutes and smashed the

A PICTORIAL GUIDE TO ORTHODOXY ON A SCREEN OF HOLY ICONS

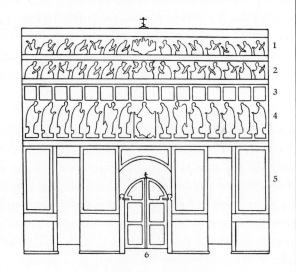

1. *Old Testament Patriarchs*

2. *Old Testament Prophets*

3. *Scenes from the lives of Christ and Mary*

4. *The Last Judgment*

5. *Locally important saints and angels*

6. *The Royal Doors*

Standing between the sanctuary and the congregation in every Russian church, the iconostasis, an elaborate altar screen, tells an illustrated story of the Bible. Each row of icons has its traditional place on the screen. The third row always pictures the events in the lives of Christ and Mary that are celebrated as holy days; the fourth row always depicts Christ, flanked by Mary, John the Baptist, archangels and saints. Separating the worshipers from the sanctuary, the iconostasis represents the division between the divine and the human worlds. The opening of the Royal Doors in its center symbolically unites the two.

clowns' masks out in the field, I alone, against a great number. I took from them two great bears; one I struck senseless, and the other I set loose in the fields. Because of this Vasily Petrovich Sheremetov, who was sailing down the Volga to Kazan, to assume the office of governor, summoned me aboard his ship. He upbraided me and ordered me to bless his son Matthew, whose face was shaven. But I did not bless him and reprimanded him from the Scriptures when I looked upon his lewd countenance. In great wrath the nobleman commanded that I should be thrown into the Volga."

There are two points of religious interest buried in Avvakum's paragraph, illustrating the two facets of the movement he led. Bears, in old pagan Russia, were regarded as supernatural creatures, demigods. In attacking the seemingly innocent dancing bears, Avvakum was striking a blow for Christ against the still-surviving forces of darkness. In refusing to bless the beardless son of the nobleman, Avvakum was at once upholding old Muscovite ritualism and protesting against heretical ideas from the West, symbolized for him by the shaven face.

In Siberia Avvakum was almost constantly tortured by czarist officers, who attempted to kill him by freezing, starvation and beating; for 12 years he was imprisoned in a hole in the ground; yet he survived, eventually made his way back to Moscow, and in 1682 was burned at the stake.

Superficially, it would appear that Avvakum, who has been described as "a man of great heart but narrow mind," suffered simply for the sake of the old ritualism and a puritanical ethic. In fact, the issues for which the Old Believers fought were far more important. The Old Believers—most of whom fled toward the Russian frontiers—were in fundamental opposition to serfdom, Muscovite autocracy and to Westernization. Besides, they took very seriously the idea that if "the third Rome" fell into heresy, the rule of Antichrist and the end of the world were close at hand. The enforced changes in ritualism convinced them that this was indeed the case, and they came to a horrendous conclusion: the Czar—or corporately, the whole czarist dynasty—was Antichrist. Because of this apocalyptic conclusion, the Old Believers saw but one escape: when the minions of Antichrist, the Czar's police, came to persecute them, suicide was imperative. Late in the 17th Century tens of thousands of Old Believers locked themselves in their churches, set the buildings afire, and died in mass immolations.

The schism between the Old Believers and those who were willing to accept changes in the rituals was never healed, and the Church, seriously weakened by its internal split, never recovered its national prestige. During the reign of Peter the Great the Patriarchate was abolished and the Church became simply another bureau in the autocratic mechanism. Many clergymen were reduced to the pathetic status of apologists for the state; in fact they were ordered to become spies. By Peter's order, priests who heard "seditious" remarks during the sacrament of confession were even instructed to report them in detail to the police.

Russian Christianity, to be sure, did not die, nor were the magnificent ideals of kenoticism ever forgotten. The lower clergy often benefited, in the eyes of the people, from their underdog position. The greatest of Russian writers, Dostoevsky, repeatedly sounded forth the trumpet in the 19th Century. In his *Diary* he wrote, "Whoever wants to be highest in the kingdom of God must become everyone's servant. This is how I understand the Russian purpose." Or again, in the words of Father Zosima in *The Brothers Karamazov*, "God will save his own people, for great is Russia in her humility." Doubtless at this moment, 1,000 years after the conversion, there are Russians who are still secretly writing or saying substantially the same thing.

A PORTRAIT OF TENDERNESS *is revealed in this copy of Russia's most famous icon, Our Lady of Vladimir.*

IMAGES OF A NATION'S SOUL

Of all Russia's cultural achievements, none reflected so brilliantly the deepest feelings of her people as her icons. These sacred images of Christ, Mary, saints and angels, rendered in stunning colors in mosaics or on painted wood panels, mirrored the devotion of a country where religious fervor was a fact of daily life. Icons gleamed from the walls of every Russian Orthodox church and hung in every Russian household, from the czar's palace to the meanest peasant hut. Often they were credited with miraculous powers: divine intervention by Our Lady of Vladimir, the most celebrated icon in all Russia, was believed to have protected Moscow on three different occasions from invasions by foreign armies.

A HERITAGE OF HOLY ARTISTRY

The first icon of the Mother and Child, according to Orthodox tradition, was a portrait painted by St. Luke, the Greek physician who wrote one of the Gospels. Byzantine Greece was, in fact, the cultural forebear from which Russia inherited the art of icon making. When Vladimir, the Prince of Kiev, was converted to Christianity in 988, he hired Byzantine craftsmen to build churches and to adorn their interiors with mosaics and paintings of religious figures. It was from these icons that early Russian artists adopted both the sacred heroes and the distinctive style of the Byzantines.

But subtle changes soon modified the look of icons wrought by Russian craftsmen. As the art filtered north to Novgorod and Moscow, vigorous figures—often in Slavic dress—began replacing the stiffer, formalized Byzantine models. The brilliant reds and greens of their costumes seemed to burn like embers against their golden backgrounds.

Despite these changes, Russian icons lost none of their deeply religious qualities. Not only were finished icons consecrated by priests, but even the paints and brushes were ceremoniously blessed, and the painters themselves were believed to have worked under divine inspiration.

A BYZANTINE ST. DEMETRIOS, *revered as a champion of militant Christianity, is shown in a mosaic from an 11th Century church in Kiev. The austere pose reflects the influence of Byzantine style.*

Сни велвкомчв ГЕОРГИ

A RUSSIAN ST. GEORGE *slays a dragon, symbolic of evil, and rescues a princess in this 15th Century icon in robust Novgorod style. As an angel crowns the saint, God blesses him from a heavenly cloud.*

FIERY PROTECTOR OF THE HOME

The family icon, which hung enshrined in every Russian peasant's cottage, served as a talisman to ward off the dark forces of nature. A favorite subject for family icons was the Biblical prophet Elijah. This Old Testament figure inspired special reverence in Russian farmers because he supposedly controlled the forces of nature, among them the rainfall that watered their crops and the fire that would frequently destroy their wooden houses. They knew by heart the stories of Elijah's miracles—how ravens brought him food in time of drought, and how an angelic coachman conveyed him to heaven in a fiery chariot *(right)*, as he dropped his mantle to his successor Elisha.

Illiterate peasants handed down these legendary tales, like the icons that depicted them, from generation to generation. For the great mass of Russians, in fact, the only meaningful records of Biblical events were the icons themselves, whose painted scenes formed a testament in pictures for a populace unable to read.

NATIVITY

ANNUNCIATION

BAPTISM

TRANSFIGURATION

RAISING OF LAZARUS

A CALENDAR OF SACRED FEASTS

In every Russian church, a special row of icons depicted events from the life of Christ which were observed as the year's main holidays. Ranged across the elaborate screen standing between the congregation and the altar, they showed New Testament events in conventional tableaux adopted from Byzantine tradition. In a country where all holidays were religious, each one meant a day of feasts and ceremonies.

Easter, the celebration of the Resurrection, was the most exuberantly joyful holiday of all. Ceremonies began with Palm Sunday, when both the Czar and the Patriarch of the Church paraded through Moscow attended by priests who carried icons and crosses. On Easter morning, all Russia went to church, and then celebrated with a day of drinking and banqueting.

CRUCIFIXION

RESURRECTION

ASCENSION

THE INTIMATE WATCH OF GUARDIAN ANGELS

Every proper Christian in Russia had a guardian saint or angel to whom he confided his hopes, addressed his prayers and turned for protection in time of danger. Often he carried a miniature icon of his patron in his pocket; he regarded it not merely as a likeness in paint and wood, but as an actual physical incarnation of a divine presence. When he took the icon out to look at it, he believed the figure was able to look back at him through painted eyes.

Often a person's patron was also his namesake; a man named Michael invoked St. Michael in his prayers and celebrated the feast of St. Michael in place of his own birthday. In many cases an icon of the saint hung over his bed during his lifetime; when he died, his family often had a commemorative icon painted and displayed in the local church.

A COMPASSIONATE PROTECTOR, *the Archangel Michael (left) was the patron saint of princes in battle. Though the leader of heavenly armies, he appears in a tender mood in this icon by the master Andrei Rublev.*

A MINISTERING SPIRIT, *the Archangel Gabriel is shown at right in the strongly primitive Novgorod style. Because Gabriel announced the birth of Christ to Mary, he was venerated as the protector of women in childbirth.*

A NATIONAL PATRON'S LIFE OF CHARITY

No religious figure was so dear to the hearts of the Russian people as St. Nicholas. The Fourth Century Archbishop of Myra in Turkey, Nicholas was believed to have performed miraculous deeds of charity: curing the sick, saving mariners from drowning, bringing dead children to life and snatching condemned prisoners from the executioner's sword.

Icons of St. Nicholas often depicted in detail these acts of kindness, thus serving as visual object lessons of the generous Christian life. In most Western countries he became the patron saint of Christmas, but the Russians adopted him as the protector of children, the poor and all travelers, and eventually as the patron saint of Russia itself. Their veneration for him is reflected in an old Russian saying: "If God dies, we still have St. Nicholas."

CALMING A STORM (left), St. Nicholas saves three seafarers from drowning, in a detail from an icon of the Novgorod school. When waves threatened to capsize their tiny boat, the men prayed to the saint, who suddenly appeared aboard to guide them to safety.

A HISTORY OF HOLINESS, the life of St. Nicholas is depicted around a portrait of the saint, clad in bishop's robes. Between scenes of his birth, ordination and death (top and bottom rows), he is shown ministering to people menaced by danger, poverty, illness and injustice.

6

"THE TIME OF TROUBLES"

When Ivan the Terrible died in 1584 he left no likely successor. In a moment of rage the half-mad Czar had killed his only promising son, who was also named Ivan, with a blow of his pointed staff. Two other sons survived, a mentally retarded weakling named Fedor, who inherited the crown by default, and an infant called Dimitry. The latter, a child of Ivan's seventh wife, had no real status in the line of succession: Orthodox canon law permitted but three wives; children of the fourth, let alone the seventh, were not recognized as legitimate heirs. Still the name Dimitry, in view of what was soon to happen, must be writ large.

Czar Fedor was far removed from the world of Russian reality. He spent most of his waking hours in monotonous prayer, and he took a special delight in listening to church bells. He could not hear, much less understand, the rumblings of approaching catastrophe in the land. Ivan's political terrorizing and his disastrous wars against Poland and Sweden had further impoverished the country and left the people, high and low, in a mood of bitter discontent. Even the service gentry, who had benefited from redistribution of the land under the *oprichnina*, were in a sorry plight. Their estates had been depopulated by the flight, in ever larger numbers, of peasants seeking relief from debt and local tyranny, and now had small value. And many urban merchants and craftsmen, borne down by taxes, were following the peasants to the frontiers.

Fedor "ruled" for 14 years, during which time the dwindling ranks of the boyars began their resurgence against autocracy. They were at first too disunited to be strong enough to control the throne. The true power fell to one of the recently elevated service gentry, a semiliterate but politically astute man of Tartar descent named Boris Godunov, whose sister was married to Fedor. Skillfully exploiting this connection, Godunov made himself the de facto ruler of Russia. In his struggle for dominance he defeated the family of the Romanovs, who had provided Ivan the Terrible with his beloved first wife, Anastasia, and who still enjoyed wide popularity among the people.

In 1591, while Fedor reigned and Boris Godunov ruled, there occurred an accidental death, or perhaps a murder, which was destined to stir up an

THE EMPTY THRONE *of Ivan the Terrible was not adequately filled for 29 years after his death. His weak son Fedor succeeded him, but a destructive power struggle went on until Michael Romanov emerged as czar in 1613.*

incredibly complex political turmoil in Russia and, eventually, to provide material for two great works of art—Alexander Pushkin's play and Modest Moussorgsky's opera, both called *Boris Godunov*. The half-forgotten young Prince Dimitry, living with his mother under guard in the small city of Uglich, was found mysteriously dead with his throat cut. Official investigators, appointed by Godunov, reported that the 10-year-old boy had been playing with a knife, had suffered an epileptic seizure, and had killed himself. No evidence has ever been found to refute the findings, but Dimitry's death was, at the least, a convenient occurrence for Godunov. The child might never have been recognized as a claimant to the throne; Czar Fedor was only 30 at the time, and might well have sired an unchallengeable successor; yet many Russians were later willing to believe, with Pushkin and Moussorgsky, that Dimitry had been killed at Godunov's order.

As it developed, Fedor produced no heir, and at his death in 1598 the more-than-600-year-old dynasty of the Varangian princes came to an end. Boris Godunov was elected czar by a *Zemsky Sobor*, which in this instance functioned with considerable democratic power. Godunov was a popular choice, experienced in government, and by all accounts an honorable man who wished to serve his country well. Nevertheless his accession to the throne marked the beginning of the wildest and most confusing period in all Russian history, the 15-year "Time of Troubles."

Both Pushkin and Moussorgsky, in their dramatic works, treat the story of Boris Godunov as high tragedy, and the actual events of his short reign curiously (and retroactively) support Oscar Wilde's bon mot that nature imitates art. If it is taken as true that Godunov did cause the murder of Dimitry, expiation of the dark crime is a dramatic necessity. In tragic drama, retribution would be exacted by fate, however the protagonist strove to avoid it. The real-life Godunov, soon after becoming czar, tried to bring about stability by destroying the boyars, including the Romanovs; but some survived, and from them would spring a line greater than his own. Hopeful of bringing enlightenment to Russia, Godunov attempted to set up a university in Moscow but was forced by the Church, which opposed "foreign contamination," to abandon the plan. Thwarted, he sent several young Russians to study abroad; nothing of note came of that. In 1601, fate further tightened the noose; drought and then famine ravaged the land. Despite Godunov's efforts to collect and distribute food, perhaps as many as a million people perished. Armed mobs of desperate men began sweeping through central Russia, doing battle with the regular army and pillaging towns and estates where food or valuables might be found.

Amidst this chaos there arose widespread rumors —very likely created and spread by boyars who wished to get rid of Godunov, whom they considered low-born—that young Prince Dimitry had not, after all, been killed at Uglich. The assassins, so the rumors went, had bungled their assignment and knifed the wrong boy. Presently there appeared a youth who claimed to be the true prince; he is known in Russian history as "False Dimitry." False Dimitry sought recognition and help in Poland, and succeeded with some of the nobility and, particularly, with the Jesuits, who exacted from him a promise that he would become a Catholic and Romanize Russia if he gained the throne.

In 1604, with a small band of Polish warriors, Cossacks and peasants, he invaded Russia and was warmly received, especially by the swarms of discontented migrants in the south. Boris Godunov fought him, and in 1605 was in sight of victory when fate intervened for the last time. Apparently in robust health, Godunov suddenly sickened and died, and False Dimitry entered Moscow in triumph to be crowned czar.

The young ruler, whoever he was, reigned for only 13 months. His large retinue of Catholic Poles antagonized the Muscovites. Led by the powerful boyar, Prince Vasily Shuisky, Russian soldiers and townsfolk slaughtered the Poles and executed False Dimitry. Shuisky became czar by popular acclamation, and False Dimitry's remains, reduced to a more convenient size by burning, were stuffed into a cannon and fired in the general direction of Poland. Thus, only 22 years after the death of Ivan the Terrible, the old aristocracy had again taken over power in Muscovy.

What occurred during the remainder of the "Time of Troubles," from 1606 to 1613, may be summarized briefly. Czar Vasily Shuisky—the "boyar czar"—had no base of power among the service gentry or common people, who remained in a continuous state of unrest. In the south a former slave named Ivan Bolotnikov led a mass revolt of Cossacks, runaway peasants and vagabonds, directed not merely against the Czar but against all authority and all holders of valuable private property. Bolotnikov's vast mob reached the gates of Moscow before it was repulsed. Later, other pretenders to the throne were put forth, including a False Peter and a second False Dimitry. The latter set up his headquarters in the town of Tushino, only a few miles from Moscow, and for a time the state had two czars, with the allegiance of the population about equally divided between them.

In 1610 Vasily Shuisky was deposed by a boyar council and False Dimitry II was murdered by one of his lieutenants in a quarrel over money. Russia then, and for three years thereafter, had no czar, and in effect no government, except for an ineffectual huddle of frightened boyars who called themselves a duma.

Claims to the Russian throne advanced by the West added to the Russian predicament. Sweden declared war, marched on Novgorod and put forth Prince Philip, brother of King Gustavus II of Sweden, as a candidate for the czardom. Poland, considerably more menacing, seized Smolensk and other Russian territories, reoccupied Moscow, and attempted to establish Sigismund III, King of Poland, as ruler. Thus assaulted by external enemies, riddled by rebellions in her own territory, bankrupt, and plagued by famine and disease, Russia was on the point of national disintegration.

That Russia did not perish can be attributed only to the strength and somewhat mystic communion of her people. The rally of the people began in the Orthodox Church, chiefly among leaders in Moscow and the hallowed Holy Trinity-St. Sergius Monastery, who sent couriers across the land appealing both to patriotism and to religious faith: Holy Russia, the "Third Rome," the last bastion of "true" Christianity, must not be allowed to fall before the Catholic "heretics" of the West.

The effectiveness of this appeal was exemplified by the response of the people of one small city, Nizhny Novgorod. There the people gave one third of all their possessions to finance a crusade. Other towns and cities quickly responded and soon a great national army—which to the Poles must have appeared to spring spontaneously out of the Russian earth—was marching on Moscow. With its supply and organization managed by so obscure a man as a poor butcher, Kuzma Minin, and its military operations commanded by the high-born Prince Dimitry Pozharsky, the national army could not be defeated. Praying, fasting, implacable, it wiped out the Polish garrison in Moscow and then encamped in and near the city, so strong a force that neither Poland nor Sweden had the stomach to challenge it.

The national army was also the national government; containing elements of all classes, from boyar to peasant, the army soon convened the Zemsky Sobor for the purpose of electing a czar. The choice fell upon a 16-year-old boy, whose name might have wrung a sigh from the ghost of Boris Godunov: Michael Romanov.

Although many powers brought about his selection, Michael's principal qualifications were the esteem in which the Muscovite masses held his family, and his acceptability to the Cossacks. The latter had fought on both sides during the recent wars, and had to be placated at all costs. Young Michael's link by marriage to the defunct line of Ivan the Terrible also counted heavily. Moreover, his very youth was in his favor; he had been too young to participate in the swirling disasters of the Time of Troubles.

Praising God for their deliverance, the Russians reverently crowned their new Czar in 1613. He and his descendants would re-establish autocracy and reign for more than 300 years, until the last of the Romanovs was cut down in the revolution of 1917. To be sure, the mere installation of Michael did not bring Russia's woes to an end. The country remained bankrupt, and settlements with the aggressive Poles and Swedes were yet to be made. However, by ceding territories in the West and by paying heavy indemnities that the state could scarcely afford, Russia by 1618 bought a breathing space and was able to begin the mending of her internal ruin.

Michael was not a strong czar, nor was his son Alexis or his grandson Fedor III. It was not until 1689, when Peter the Great was crowned, that another gigantic figure ruled the land. Russian history during most of the 17th Century is therefore not concerned chiefly with individuals in the Kremlin but with developments that took place with little czarist leadership or control.

During the early years of Michael's reign the Zemsky Sobor—at his request—met frequently to advise him, and briefly gave promise of developing into a parliament similar to those in the West. However, Russia was not prepared for a form of government so different from the old autocracy, and inevitably the Zemsky Sobor began to disintegrate. Its various competing factions, representing both the aristocratic and the service nobility, both the wealthy merchants of Moscow and the poorer traders of other cities, were filled with mutual antagonism. As its disunion increased, the embryonic "parliament" met only at widening intervals until mid-century, when it quietly ceased to be an effective force.

The boyar duma still existed under the early Romanovs, but it too was riddled with old quarrels and jealousies, and in any case its membership had been so altered in the days of the oprichnina that it was unable to unite as a counterweight to czarist authority. Thus it slowly came about that autocracy, which Ivan the Great and Ivan the Terrible had struggled to establish by diplomacy and the sword, was restored to the feeble Romanovs by default. Although in later centuries Russia would produce political philosophers of bewildering variety, in the 17th Century the country had no such men, and could only look to the past, to a system of government that, for all its hideous abuses and imperfections, was all Russia knew.

The restoration of czarist absolutism was accompanied by the slow, relentless establishment of a caste system in Muscovite society. No monarch, it would seem, ever sat down and made definite plans as to what this system should be; it simply developed gradually, without direction, out of the problems and needs of the state.

The greatest of these needs was a stable population of peasants, small businessmen and craftsmen, firmly rooted in the countryside and towns, which could perform three functions: work the lands of the officer-class service gentry, pay taxes and furnish common soldiers for the army. But the population of Muscovy was anything but stable—since the time of Ivan the Terrible, peasants in ever-increasing numbers had been fleeing to the fron-

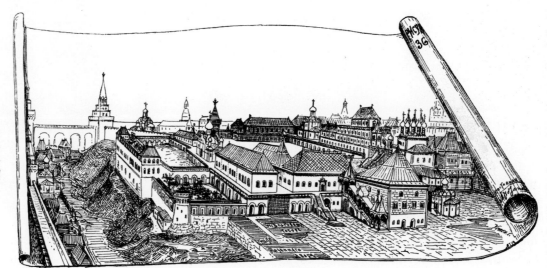

THE HEART OF THE KREMLIN *is shown as it appeared in the 17th Century, after the lofty palace (far right, between onion-domed churches) had been renovated for the Romanovs.*

tiers or quietly absconding to new homesteads where, they hoped, the census taker and the tax collector could not find them. A surprisingly large number of people, including impoverished service gentry and merchants, voluntarily sold themselves into slavery—as "non-persons," slaves were not subject to conscription or taxation. Many slaves made advantageous deals with the rich monasteries, carrying on their former occupations, under the supervision of the monks, with more profit and liberty than they had enjoyed as "free" men.

The growing scarcity of laboring men and taxpayers created difficulties for both the landlords and the czars. In the late 16th and early 17th Centuries, repeated attempts were made to prevent the flight of peasants and townsfolk, and to make their capture easier, but still the exodus continued. (At one time, on an estate personally owned by Czar Alexis Romanov, it was found that the occupants of 481 out of 664 homesteads had run away.) Desperate for workers, landlords competed with one another in offering easy terms or outright bribes to induce peasants to work for them. Prince I. N. Romanov, uncle of Czar Michael, organized armed bands to kidnap field hands for his estates. In this competition it was the poorer—and therefore more numerous—group of landlords who suffered most, and they called loudly on the Kremlin for help.

In 1649 Czar Alexis and his advisers arranged a great codification of the laws, ostensibly so that "to all the classes of the Muscovite state from the greatest to the least, law and justice shall be equal in all things." In fact, however, the Code of 1649 was designed to keep under Muscovite domination the peasants, taxpayers and recruits required by the government. Serfdom was not defined by the Code—it never was, in any Russian law—but the fact emerged plainly enough. The right of a peasant to depart from his landlord, merely theoretical though it may have been until that time, was now formally abolished. Moreover, the landbound status of the peasant became hereditary; sons could not leave the households of their fathers. Townsfolk, as well, were bound to their homesteads, under threat of torture, exile or death. The right of selling oneself into slavery was also abolished—or as the Russian historian V. O. Kluchevsky has acidly observed, "freedom became an obligation backed up by the knout."

The Code of 1649 failed to halt the running away of peasants but in its ambiguities and omissions it gave the landlords the license to reduce the peasants to actual slavery. By the beginning of the 18th Century it came to be tacitly accepted that peasants were bound not to the land, but to the person of the landlord; he could do with them what he

wished—buy them, sell them, use them as tokens in gambling, or, after whimsical trial, put them to death. The Code did not set forth specifically what the functions of the various castes in Muscovite society were to be, but it formed a basis, together with other laws and the general hardening of custom. Government servitors, whether military or bureaucratic, would remain in their roles, and these roles tended to become hereditary. Wealthy merchants and poor tradesmen, clergy and craftsmen, were, alike, to remain fixed in their positions, and their children inherited the same functions—though it was possible for some brilliant or stupid men to move up or down within the pyramidal structure. Through all this the czar remained always at the top and the serfs (perhaps 80 per cent of the population) always at the bottom.

While Muscovy slowly set its social structure in order, disorder and war flared in the south. The Cossacks of the Don, who had repeatedly defied the landlords and the czars, were not the only such men who inhabited the steppe. To the west of them, spread along the lower Dnieper, was an equally ferocious and independent band known as the Zaporogian Cossacks. (Their fortress headquarters were on an island—"below the rapids," or *za porogi*.)

The region occupied by the Zaporogian Cossacks lay in the center of the Ukraine, the homeland of the "Little Russians," and had successively been part of old Kievan Russia, the empire of the Mongols and the Lithuanian state. Since 1569, when Lithuania was effectively absorbed by Poland at the Union of Lublin, the Zaporogians had technically been subject to Polish rule—although they gave no evidence of being aware of the fact. Magnificent and fearless fighters, they assaulted the Crimean Tartars, the Turks, the Poles and Muscovites, as if for the fun of it, shouting their battle-cry *"Volnitsa!"*—"Liberty!"—as they did so. Of course it was only their own liberty to plunder or to murder that they prized, but that did not detract from their valor.

Like the Cossacks of the Don, the Zaporogians were Orthodox in religion and eastern Slavic, but most of them had come from the Ukraine rather than from the forests of the northeast. Numbering in the thousands, they were led by a freely elected commander called a *hetman*, who in turn was responsible to a general assembly in which all could participate. Their greatest delight was in physical combat, and to keep themselves fit for this they scorned the "soft" family life—women were regarded as occasional playthings and were not admitted, on pain of death, to the Cossack stronghold on the Dnieper.

By the mid-17th Century the Zaporogian host had grown to enormous size, and the Cossacks, despite their lip service to the equality of all men, had become divided into two classes. The upper class consisted of the established leaders, many of whom possessed considerable wealth and were "registered" by the Polish king—the registration placing them approximately on a level with the minor Polish nobility. The lower and far larger class contained "naked" men, peasants who had recently fled into the eastern Ukraine with only such belongings as they could carry. The flight of the naked was caused by conditions in the Union of Lublin—Catholicism was beginning to be established as the state religion, Orthodoxy was being suppressed, and Polish institutions, including serfdom, were being forced on the peasants.

Despite their privileged position, the registered Cossacks were in strong sympathy with the fugitives from Poland. In a series of wars and uprisings, the Cossack hetman, Bogdan Khmelnitsky, managed to fight Poland to a stalemate, and in 1653 he offered to put his people and his territory under the protection of Moscow. After some hesitation, in the full knowledge that an agreement with Khmelnitsky would provoke war with Poland, Czar Alexis in 1654 accepted the proposal. Ukrainian and Russian historians still argue to this day about the nature of the agreement. The Ukrainians maintain that Khmelnitsky did not approach Alexis as a supplicant; that his intention went no further than the setting up of a semiautonomous state that would defer to Moscow in matters of defense and foreign policy but that would otherwise remain independent. The Russians, for their part, hold that Khmelnitsky accepted complete subjugation.

In the inevitable Russo-Polish war that followed, the Czar's troops performed surprisingly well. All of the Ukraine east of the Dnieper became part of Muscovy, together with the cities of Kiev and Smolensk on the west bank of the river. Thus, after more than four centuries of separation, the Little Russians—as the Ukrainians were called—were reunited with their Great Russian brothers. The reunion, however, did not prove to be a happy one. During their long separation the Ukrainians had developed a partially Westernized culture, and the ways of their neighbors to the east seemed strange to them. Later, when the czars clamped down their autocratic rule on the region, the Ukrainians felt that they had been betrayed; it was not for this, they felt, that their great hero Khmelnitsky had fought. In these circumstances lies one important source of the strong sense of nationalism that Little Russians still feel to this day. As late as 1941, when German troops swept into the Ukraine, a number of Russians actually greeted them as liberators.

Although Bogdan Khmelnitsky occupies a revered place in the memory of Ukrainians (his first name means "gift of God"), the greatest hero in all the history of Cossackdom was a drunken, illiterate man named Stenka (little Stephen) Razin. Throughout Russia, folksongs about him are still sung, and in the passage of centuries legend has made him an almost supernatural figure. He could, it is said, charm poisonous snakes to make them harmless; needing warriors to help him, he had only to throw a chip from a lime tree into the Volga, where it would turn into a galley full of armed men. According to the legends, Razin buried treasures in secret places all along the river, and, long after his death, superstitious peasants believed that he still roamed the land and would help them in their troubles.

In one of the most widely known of old Russian ballads, Stenka Razin is credited with a gesture that was typically Cossack. Having captured a beautiful Persian girl and spent only one night with her, he hears his men murmuring that he is becoming soft. "In a fellowship of free men, never shall a quarrel rise. Volga, Mother Volga, take the beauty as your prize," he says—and with that, not even glancing backward, he throws the girl into the river to drown.

In the Volga basin many place names still honor him—near the city of Saratov, for example, there is a hill called Razin. According to popular belief, a man who climbs this hill at night will hear the secret message Razin has left for the peasants: a call to class war.

Razin, a Cossack of the Don, began his career in 1667 as a pirate. Assembling a band of poor men who had nothing to lose, he built small warships on the Volga, sailed south into the Caspian Sea and raided the coasts of Persia, returning with a huge cargo of booty. Almost at once he became a popular leader of great stature, attracting thousands of Cossacks and peasants to his side. With this nondescript band of followers, Razin turned north to march against Moscow. En route he was joined by non-Russian men of the eastern frontier, Moslem tribesmen of the Bashkir, Mari, Chuvash and Mordva, all of whom had good reason to quarrel with Moscow; their lands were relentlessly being taken from them in the course of Russian expansion into Asia.

Stenka Razin was ignorant of politics, and at best could only lead an uprising, not inspire a social revolution. In several respects he resembled Bolotnikov, the ex-slave who had led a rabble to Moscow during the Time of Troubles, but Razin's appeal was far broader and deeper. The countless legends that he inspired, and his extraordinary ability to attract followers, suggest what the man was: the embodiment of two raw emotions, rage and frustration, that the people could not articulate. Razin seems never to have had the slightest intention of installing himself as czar or to have had ambitions to become a regional overlord. Wealth had no particular attraction for him—even at the height of his power he lived, as the poorest Cossacks did, in a sod hut. His appeals were of the simplest kind—he attacked landlords and government officials, and conjured up dim visions of a society of "brothers."

As he advanced northward, Razin sent outriders ahead of him, calling on the serfs and working classes to revolt, and everywhere the exhortation was eagerly obeyed. When he reached Astrakhan the fortified city was already his—laborers, street cleaners, boatmen, house servants and common soldiers had turned against their masters, broken open the jails, and seized and burned the files of the tax collectors. From Astrakhan, Razin moved on to Tsaritsyn (now Volgograd) and captured it with ease. Other cities and towns all along the Volga blazed with rebellion. By 1670 Razin had 200,000 men at his back, and as he approached Moscow there were leaders in the city who believed that it might be better to offer him the traditional Russian welcome of bread and salt rather than to fight him.

However, Razin's men did not constitute an army—the only skilled fighting units among his followers were those of the Don Cossacks. The Czar's forces, on the other hand, included several disciplined regiments, armed with imported weapons and trained by Western officers. In a brief battle the rebels were smashed and, although Razin fled to the south, he was captured and taken in chains to Moscow. There the Czar's inventive torturers put him to a prolonged death; they broke his bones one by one, then quartered him alive. During his public ordeal he made no outcry and he refused to acknowledge that he was guilty of any crime. His stubborn endurance, a quality deeply admired by all Russians, lies close to the heart of his legend.

The backwardness of 17th Century Russia becomes strikingly clear in a comparison of Stenka Razin with two of his contemporaries in England —Oliver Cromwell and John Milton. Cromwell, with a clear vision of government, law and society, led the Puritan Revolution with great skill; Milton, in his brilliant writings, expounded and defended it. The naive and inarticulate Razin achieved only a few slogans and suffered disastrous defeat. Ultimately in Russia it would take men who might be called "university Cossacks" to overthrow the czars. To produce such men Russia had to be brought into closer contact with the West. Ironically, it was Peter the Great, the supreme autocrat born in the year after Razin's death, who was presently to make Westernization the grail and the garrote of those who came after him.

RUSSIA'S LEGENDARY FOUNDER, *the Varangian Rurik, arrived in Novgorod in 862 to rule the Slavs.*

HEROES, SAINTS AND ROGUES

Russia came of age in the eight centuries between Rurik, the Scandinavian prince who is said to have founded the nation's first dynasty in the Ninth Century, and Peter the Great (1672-1725), the first modern czar. The country grew in three great surges: first, the Russians' discovery of themselves as a people, unified by the Orthodox Church, with Kiev as their center; second, the sharpening sense of nationhood that followed the Mongol invasions; and finally the establishment of Moscow as the seat of power. The actors in this drama comprised a colorful cast—conquerors, idealists, strong-willed women, impostors and greedy rogues.

In the Ninth and Tenth Centuries, tough warrior-lords and Christian converts transformed the city of Kiev into the nucleus of the Russian state

RUSSIA'S FIRST RULER, *Oleg pushed out from Novgorod, took strategic Kiev in 879, subjugated nearby tribes and negotiated a lucrative trade treaty with the Byzantines that made Kiev an important commercial center.*

A FORMIDABLE COUPLE, *Igor and Olga aggressively extended Kiev's power. When Igor was murdered by tax-burdened subjects, Olga avenged his death brutally, but as regent she proved to be a wise and daring leader. She was later canonized as Russia's first influential convert to the Christian faith.*

THE GREAT LAW-GIVER, *Yaroslav the Wise, took power after a fratricidal struggle. Kievan Russia reached its zenith during his enlightened reign. He warned his sons to live in peace, lest they "bring to ruin the land," but they fell to fighting fiercely among themselves soon after his death.*

A PRINCELY CONVERT, *Vladimir gave up paganism and his concubines to become Russia's first Christian ruler. Decreeing baptism for all Kievans, he put the nation on the road to Orthodoxy.*

TWO MISSIONARY MONKS, *the Byzantines Cyril and Methodius devised the Slavs' first alphabet, providing the basis for a unifying Russian literature.*

In the 13th and 14th Centuries, fierce Mongol khans reduced
Russia to vassalage, but a few princes kept
the sense of nationhood alive, and finally threw off the invaders' yoke

A RUTHLESS WARRIOR, *Genghis Khan sent his conquering horde smashing out of central Asia, routing a Russian army in 1223. A tyrant with paradoxical visions of vanquishing the world and diffusing learning, peace and justice, Genghis Khan opened the door to the Mongol occupation of Russia.*

GENGHIS' GRANDSON, *the Mongol Batu Khan, in 1237-1240 crossed over the Urals, burned Riazan, razed Kiev and settled in the steppe to collect tribute from the Russian princes.*

ALEXANDER NEVSKY

IVAN I

DIMITRY DONSKOY

THREE RUSSIAN PRINCES, *pursuing various strategies, kept the Russians together as a people despite Mongol domination. Alexander Nevsky defended Russia's frontier against the Swedes at the Neva River even as Kiev fell to Batu. By submitting to Mongol rule, Nevsky helped save Novgorod from Kiev's fate. Moscow's wily Ivan I (called "Moneybag") fought the khans' battles and collected their taxes to curry favor, strengthening his principality's position. Dimitry Donskoy was the first to defy the conquerors outright; he defeated them on the Don in 1380, puncturing the myth of Mongol invincibility.*

THE LAST INVADER, *Tamerlane waged civil war among the Mongols and the struggle gave his enemies time to mobilize. When finally he marched on the Russians, their strength led him to retreat without attacking Moscow.*

127

Moscow became Russia's seat of power, but 16th Century battles
for the throne brought on the "Time of Troubles"

THE GREAT EXPANSIONIST, *Ivan III added*
Novgorod to Moscow's domain, ended
subservience to the Mongols in 1480 and
assumed the title "Sovereign of all Russia."

A FEEBLE-MINDED CZAR, *Fedor inherited the*
unrest stirred up by his father, Ivan the Terrible.
Fedor's brother-in-law, Boris Godunov,
was the real ruler during Fedor's 14-year reign.

THE "TWO DIMITRYS" *added to Russia's instability. The "Real Dimitry," Fedor's brother, died in childhood, amid rumors that Godunov had killed him. Twelve years later, in 1603, an adventurer appeared, claiming that he was Dimitry and alive. Godunov's son and heir was murdered and "False Dimitry" (bottom) took the throne. But within a year he in turn was killed by resentful Muscovites.*

REAL DIMITRY

AN AMBITIOUS INTERLOPER, *Boris Godunov succeeded Fedor. He used cruelty to entrench himself as czar and died barely in time to escape being overthrown.*

A WILY PATRIARCH, *Philaret was the first Romanov to rule Russia, although his son actually was czar. The dynasty, to endure for 300 years, ended the "Time of Troubles."*

FALSE DIMITRY

In the 17th Century, an assortment of rebels, reformers and Romanov rulers played their part in moving Russia toward the age of empire it finally achieved under Peter the Great

A COSSACK REBEL, *Bogdan Khmelnitsky fought to free the Ukraine from Polish oppression and was victorious, with Russian help. In 1654 the Ukrainian Cossacks swore allegiance to the czar.*

A CHURCH REFORMER, *Nikon, Patriarch of Moscow, returned many Russian rituals to Greek Orthodox traditions, but nationalistic dissenters broke away in the lasting schism of the "Old Believers."*

A WOMAN BEHIND THE THRONE, *Princess Sophie acted as regent during the minority of two co-czars: the moronic Ivan and the precocious Peter. She controlled both: literally sitting behind their dual throne concealed by a curtain, she told them what to say.*

A PROUD COUPLE, *Alexis and Natalia are shown on a medal struck to commemorate their major achievement: the birth of their son, Peter the Great, in 1672.*

AN EXPENDABLE CZARINA, *Eudoxia Lopukhina married Peter when he was 16. Within months he left her to go back to playing war games and building ships.*

7

A VARIED PEOPLE
AND THEIR ART

From the 16th Century onward, foreign travelers came to Russia in increasing numbers and (with some notable exceptions) hastened home to write unflattering and even scurrilous accounts about the Russian people. As a rule these foreign reporters overlooked the courage, warmth and hospitality of the Russians, and made scant mention of their centuries-long struggle against invaders from East and West. Instead they almost invariably noted that the people were suspicious, secretive, untruthful and crude.

The fact is that the seeds of Russian culture that were later to burgeon into its great modern period of creativity—in music, painting, literature, drama, the dance—had been germinating for centuries when the foreign visitors started arriving. Evidences of this—the cathedrals, the incomparable icons, the beauty of the peasant crafts—were there for the foreign visitors to write about, if they had not found the scandalous more to the taste of their readers back home.

There was, indeed, some truth to their allegations. Having come tardily to Christianity and to nationhood, the Russians felt an understandable insecurity that was made all the stronger by the hostility of their neighbors and by the conviction that the West intended to subvert the Orthodox Church. Russian uneasiness was also reinforced by the experiences of the Russian merchants and traders, who often found themselves fleeced by the English and the Dutch. Although the Russians were expert in making calculations with the abacus, they could easily be deceived by false information on rates of exchange on the conversion of their weights and measures to those of Western Europe. By the 16th Century the Russians had already acquired their fateful distrust of the West, and the Westerners their scorn of everything Russian. Ivan the Terrible, in his zeal to establish contacts with England, had granted special privileges to English merchants that gave them marked advantages over their competitors among his own people, but to little avail. (At one time England looked upon Russia as a potential colony.)

Under Czar Alexis in the 17th Century an international postal system was established to improve communications with the West but, if the com-

A POTPOURRI OF PEOPLES, *from befurred Bashkirs to turbaned Tartars, was added to Russia by expansion in the 16th and 17th Centuries. Conquest and colonization brought adherents of every major religion and dozens of new ethnic strains into an empire that numbered some 14 million people.*

plaint of the Russian merchant Ivan Pososhkov is to be credited, even that attempt to be neighborly worked to the Russians' disadvantage. In 1701 Pososhkov wrote: "[Foreigners] have cut a hole from our land into their own, and from outside people can now, through this hole, observe all our political and commercial relations. This hole is the post. The harm it does to the realm is incalculable. Everything that goes on in our land is known to the whole world. The foreigners become rich by it, and Russians become poor as beggars. The foreigners always know which of our goods are cheap and which are dear, which are plentiful and which are scarce. Thereupon they bargain, and . . . in this way trade is unequal. It is a very bad thing that people know in other countries everything that happens in ours."

It was commonplace for foreigners to make the charge that the Russian people were brutish and uncultured, though it should be borne in mind that until the late 18th Century all writers—and most literate people in every country—were aristocrats to whom the common people everywhere were uncouth boors. One early 16th Century writer, the German Ambassador Sigismund von Herberstein, took the trouble to give some serious thought to the subject of Russian "brutality." Did the czarist autocrat brutalize the people, he asked, or did the brutish people make the autocracy necessary? Herberstein found no answer.

One accusation often made was that there was widespread drunkenness in Russia, and this was by no means unjustified. The German scholar Adam Olearius, who visited Moscow four times between 1634 and 1643, noted that "There is no place in the world where drunkenness is more common than in Muscovy. All, of all conditions, ecclesiastics and lay, men and women, old and young, will drink strong water at any time. . . . Nay, the great ones are not free from this vice, as for example, the Muscovite Ambassador, sent to Charles, King of Sweden, in the year 1608, who, forgetting his quality and the affairs his master had entrusted him with, took so much strong water the night before he was to have audience, that the next day being found dead in his bed, they were forced to carry him to his grave, instead of conducting him to audience."

AN EMBROIDERED IDYLL, *the fringe of a bedspread from a St. Petersburg home displays the Russian peasants' flair for beautifying useful items. The scene likens the city to Paradise.*

At another point in his account, Olearius told about a party at which a group of husbands got thoroughly intoxicated, and then were joined by their wives. "The men being got drunk, would have gone home, but the women thought it was not yet time to draw off, though invited thereto by a good number of boxes o' th' ear, and got their husbands to sit down again, and to drink roundly as before, till such time as the men being fallen down asleep on the ground, the women sat upon them, as upon benches, and drunk on till they also were forced to lie down by them."

Characteristics that are more typically Russian —and of much greater cultural significance—than a liking for alcohol are the national tendencies toward melancholy and skepticism. The melancholy is often attributed to the Russian physical environment—the interminable gray winters and the loneliness of the vast plain—and the skepticism is assumed to be a logical reaction to Russian history itself. Memories of invasions, internal wars, despotic rule, famines and plagues are not easily erased.

Tremendous physical endurance, patience and passive courage were among the more admirable Russian qualities commented on by foreign visitors, particularly as they observed the conscripted serf-soldier in war. The 19th Century French historian, Leroy-Beaulieu, saw the Russian fighting man as "the most enduring in Europe. . . . [His] capacity for suffering is unknown to the nations of the West. . . . Across the steppes of the south, marching until totally exhausted, when they would die along the roads, by the hundred thousand, with not a cry of revolt, almost without a moan or murmur. . . . And yet the Russian people are naturally the least pugnacious, the least warlike in the world."

Perhaps above all the Russian peasant was what the Englishman Sir Bernard Pares called a master of "the art of evasion." Throughout his history the Russian peasant was subject to the rule of a very small elite—at first Varangians, then Mongol officials, followed by native princes, aristocrats and foreign "experts" imported by the Romanovs. The peasant, although he did revere the czar, had no identification with the elite and little comprehension of their aims; he wanted merely to be left alone. He would agree with those in power, or at least pay whatever lip service was required, and then he would proceed to do precisely what he wished, within the limits of caution. Thus the frequent charge of slothfulness that has been brought against the Russians assumes a different light in the words of John Perry, an English engineer who went to Russia to serve Peter the Great early in the 18th Century.

"There is this instance more that I cannot but mention," said Perry, "touching the misery of these people; namely, that if any poor man be naturally ingenious, or a better workman than his neighbors in a country town or place, or be sent upon the Czar's works, he usually endeavors to conceal it, and pretends to be ignorant [for the reason] that he gets no rest, but is constantly sent for and employed, [without] suitable encouragement; but in the place thereof, if they do not please, or murmur, and are not content, they often get stripes [i.e., whipped] for their labour."

Left to himself, the peasant was inclined to cultivate his garden, to clothe himself, provide food for his family, build his house, cherish his folklore and husband his obstinacy. The rhythm of his life was marked by periods of furious labor during the short growing season, and of hibernating lassitude during the winter. The violent ebb and flow of activity, and the swings of mood connected with it, deceived many Europeans. Alternately euphoric and downcast, a Russian might not mean precisely what he said in either state.

William Richardson, an English scholar who saw Russia late in the 18th Century, said of the people: "They are bearded children. . . . They will express the most ardent affection in the most ardent language; they will express the most furious rage in the most vindictive terms . . . but those feelings subside; other interests engage his heart; he never meant to deceive you. . . . Rigid virtue may call this double-dealing; but the Russian neither intends deceit, nor thinks his conduct deceitful."

Because all houses north of the steppe, whether they were in cities or villages, were built entirely of wood, fire was the great and constant fear of the peasant, who called it "the red rooster." The superstitious peasants often painted red roosters on the walls of their houses and barns in the belief that this would ward off disaster. Between 1330 and 1453 Moscow was swept by 17 fires, all of them major. "To make a conflagration remarkable in this country," reported one visitor, "there must be at least seven or eight thousand houses consumed."

The peasants, most of whom were illiterate, had no books or records to be destroyed by the fires. Consequently whatever of their folklore there is left has been preserved by generations of storytellers who committed it to memory and passed it on to their children. Russian fairy tales are in general similar to those of Western Europe, but have a special tone and outlook not found elsewhere. The Russian witch Baba Yaga, for example, is not quite like the witches of Andersen and the Grimms. Baba Yaga lives in a house that moves about on hen's legs, its lock is actually a mouth full of sharp teeth. Baba Yaga does not fly on a broomstick, but is transported by a mortar and pestle. She eats human flesh and is served by three pairs of disembodied hands and by three horsemen who are white, black and red, to symbolize the day, the night and the dawn.

Russian folktales frequently involve real and imaginary figures in a heroic genre called *byliny*. An outstanding figure of the old *byliny* is Ilya of Murom, who was probably only legendary, but who is said to have been a knight in the service of the Grand Prince of Kiev, Vladimir. Ilya of Murom is physically no larger than ordinary men, but when he sets out to do battle with the steppe nomads he first dispatches one of them and then, using the body as a club, proceeds to demolish a whole army.

In his old age, Ilya comes to the intersection of three roads, where stones point the directions to wealth, to a wife and to death. He feels that it is too late for him to acquire a wife, and he has no interest in riches; therefore he takes the road to death. On the way he is attacked by 40,000 thieves, but angrily kills them all and returns to the crossroad to write on the stone that he had followed death but had been cheated out of it. He then takes the road toward a wife, but finds her to be a sorceress who has imprisoned a dozen noble warriors. Ilya outwits her, frees the warriors and returns to take the last road, toward wealth. At the end of it he finds a fabulous treasure, which he distributes among orphans and beggars. Poor, wifeless and unafraid, he goes on fighting for many years, until at last he is turned to stone during a great battle.

The byliny, still repeated by peasants in modern Russian, are generally without rhyme, meter or any unifying device. Nonetheless they are revealing of peasant character. Ilya's search for death, for one instance, is typically Russian in its sense of irony. The attitude of the Russian peasant as shown in his proverbs was not that of a man who feared that something would go wrong but of one who expected that it would: "The falling leaf whispers something to living men"; "God is too high and the Czar is too far"; "On a dangerous road, wear your beard over your shoulder"; "If only one evil woman lived on earth, every man would claim her as his wife";

A MUSCOVITE BOYAR

A GLOSSARY OF RUSSIAN TERMS

BOYAR	*originally a tribal leader, later a landed nobleman*
BYLINA	*an epic folk ballad, sometimes historical*
COSSACKS	*free men, living in warlike bands along frontiers*
DRUZHINA	*in early Russia, a prince's armed retinue*
DUMA	*in Kievan Russia, a prince's council of nobles*
DVOEVERIE	*the persistence of paganism among peasant converts*
GRIVNA	*a silver ingot used as an early unit of currency*
KOPECK	*a Russian coin equal to 1/100 of a ruble*
KVASS	*a popular malt brew, weaker than beer*
OPRICHNINA	*a "state within a state" organized by Ivan IV*
OPRICHNIKS	*members of Ivan's clique who ran the oprichnina*
STRELTSY	*the elite branch of the Muscovite army*
VECHE	*an early urban assembly open to all free men*
YARLYK	*a khan's warrant investing a prince in office*
ZEMSKY SOBOR	*in Muscovy, an assembly of advisers to the ruler*

"Light a candle for the Devil too: you never know"; "The little one is too small; the big one is too big; the medium one is just right—but I can't reach it"; "We don't live uphill, but downhill"; or "Fear life, not death."

Peasants—the overwhelming majority of the Russians, as of all medieval societies—were not invariably melancholy. When they had the inclination (and the money) to get drunk, they would say: "The church is near but the road is icy; the tavern is far, but I will walk very carefully." Their imagery was sharp: "Mosquitoes sing over the living, priests over the dead," or "That money-lender would tear the skin off a flea."

The tools used by artisans and laborers in Western Europe were not available to the Russian peasant. In building his house the peasant ordinarily used only one implement, an ax, but with that he was remarkably skilled. The ax served him both as saw and plane, and often as a tool for surprisingly delicate carving—he could, as the great writer Leo Tolstoy noted, even shape spoons with it. The walls of his dwelling in the forest areas were made of tree trunks, mortised at the corners and left round on the outside; within they were often hewn smooth as planks. The central feature of every one-room house was an enormous stove of baked clay; the top was kept just comfortably warm, and the stove was so large than an entire family could sleep on it in winter.

It was inaccurate to note, as many travelers did, that Russians were by inclination physically dirty. In Olearius' commentary he remarks that "baths . . . are so common in Muscovy that there is neither town nor village but has very many of them, both public and private." After visiting a Russian bath, which was not unlike the Finnish sauna, he wrote, "'Tis almost a miracle to see how their bodies, accustomed to, and hardened by cold, can endure so intense a heat, and how that, when they are not able to endure it any longer, they come out of the stoves, naked as the back of a man's hand, both men and women, and go into the cold water, or cause it to be poured on them, and in winter, how they wallow in the snow."

The peasant could afford to eat meat only rarely,

subsisting in the main on a diet of dark rye bread broken into a soup called *shchi*, of which the principal ingredient was sauerkraut. This was supplemented by frozen or salted fish, and by fresh or dried mushrooms, which grow in abundance in the moist earth of the north. At times dreadful famines swept the land—a German merchant, Konrad Bussow, wrote of one that he had witnessed in the years 1601-1604. "I swear by God that in Moscow I saw, with my own eyes, people . . . who ate grass during the summer and hay in the winter. Parents killed, prepared and cooked many of their children."

As to the clothing Russian peasants wore, a description written by Robert Ker Porter, an English artist who visited Russia early in the 19th Century, probably also fits the attire that had been worn in earlier times. "Thick swathes of rags are rolled about their legs to keep out the cold, over which they pull a pair of large and ill-constructed boots. Those who do not arrive at the luxury of these leathern defences, increase the swathings to such a bulk by wrappings and cross bandages, that their lower extremities appear more like flour sacks than the legs of men. When thus bulwarked, they stuff them into a pair of enormous shoes, made very ingeniously from the bark of the linden tree. . . . It is curious to observe how closely [their dress] resembles that worn by the English in the reign of Richard II. . . . Any one who has considered the old [sculptured] tombs in our cathedrals . . . will not doubt of the fact, but immediately perceive that the peasantry of Russia in the 19th Century, are contemporaries in fashion with those of England in the 14th."

Although outsiders took immense delight in discussing Russian sexual promiscuity—a phenomenon they had perhaps failed to observe in their own countries—the Russian family unit was in fact exceedingly close. Amid the swirl of migration and colonization, the vast emptiness of the plain, and the sense of uneasiness that Russians felt in regard to their overlords, strangers, and even their neighbors, family relationships were among the few ties upon which Russians could rely. This was true equally of the peasants and the nobility, who also received their share of abuse in the writings of foreigners.

In the peculiar structure of the Russian family lay the origins of Russian socio-political development, both under the czars and later. The German Baron von Haxthausen, who traveled in Russia in the 1830s, wrote: "The family is the national microcosm; in it reigns a perfect equality of rights. The Commune is the family enlarged. The land belongs to the family or commune; each individual has only a claim to usufruct [profits], to which all persons born in the Commune have an equal right. The land therefore is equally divided among all who live upon it, to be temporarily occupied by them. No right of inheritance exists in the children to the share of their father; each son claims an equal share with the rest, by virtue of his individual right as a member of the Commune.

"According to the traditional conviction of the people, Russia belongs to the Nation, divided into Communes, as to a single family, under its chief or father, the Czar, who has the disposal of everything and to whom implicit obedience is shown."

Although they had more education than the peasantry, the nobles were at best semiliterate until the beginning of the 18th Century. Ambassador Herberstein, who wrote the first Western account of them, noted that they made an impressive appearance in the court of Ivan the Great, in their rich robes and tall fur hats—but added that they seemed to have nothing to say. In their personal habits they were crude, and apparently an embarrassment even to Ivan the Terrible. During his reign, at any rate, there appeared a manual called the

Domostroy (The Good Householder), written by Ivan's chaplain Sylvester. The work was intended to improve the public manners of the nobility, although perhaps its most celebrated precept is: "Punish your son in his youth, and he will give you a quiet old age, and restfulness to your soul. Weaken not beating the boy, for he will not die from your striking him with the rod, but will be in better health. . . ."

In other matters, the Domostroy revealed the Russian self-consciousness, particularly in regard to foreign visitors. "Let [your wife] put on her best garment, if she receives a visitor, or is herself invited somewhere to dinner. By all means let her abstain from drinking liquor, for a drunk man is bad enough, but a drunk woman has no place in the world. . . . Enjoin your servants not to talk about other people. If they have been among strangers, and have noticed anything bad there, let them not repeat it at home. . . . Let not your servant put his finger in his nose, nor cough, nor clear his throat, nor spit."

The injunction against public spitting was apparently not taken to heart either by servants or noblemen—or so, at least, runs the account of an Englishman who wrote early in the 19th Century: "There is another custom very prevalent among the Russian nobility, which is extremely disagreeable—that of spitting on the floor. Neither fine inlaid floors, nor even Wilton carpets, oppose any obstacle to this detestable practice. The Russian noble will spit immediately before you, and rub the saliva with his foot. It is but just to say, however, that he, sometimes, retires to a corner of the room, to conceal his deposit."

Although there were many exceptions, Russian noblemen were often as cruel as they were crude. As owners of the serfs, they were also the accusers and the judges in cases at law, and their common instrument of punishment was the knout. This

BEHIND VERSAILLES' FACADE

Early Western visitors to Russia often claimed to be horrified by that country's barbarity and uncouth manners. Yet even at Louis XIV's Versailles, the center of civilized delight in the 17th Century world, life often had its crude side.

Versailles—built, like St. Petersburg, at the cost of thousands of workers' lives—took some 60 per cent of France's annual revenue to run. Yet, aside from its magnificent royal quarters and public halls, most of the rooms were dark, cold and foul-smelling; some were so small their occupants could not stand erect in them and others had no windows at all. Corridors were labyrinthine; one impecunious noblewoman, who was forgotten by the court, nearly starved to death in a garret room before she was found during a search for a new royal governess.

Guests of Louis accommodated themselves to their host's rules. Louis, like Peter the Great, refused to use a knife and fork. Moreover, according to one observer, he would sometimes "amuse himself by throwing bread pellets at the ladies, and allowing them to hurl pellets at him." One lady-in-waiting, winged by a piece of fruit, retaliated by hurling a dish of salad, complete with dressing, at the Sun King's head.

singularly vicious whip was like a flail, with a wooden handle attached to a thick strip of rawhide that had been boiled in milk until it was nearly as hard as metal. With three strokes, it has been said, an experienced wielder of the knout could kill a man. But in fact, murder was not a common form of punishment because it diminished the property of the nobleman.

The status of women in Muscovite Russia was, as Herberstein wrote, "most miserable; for they consider no woman virtuous unless she live shut up at home, and be so closely guarded that she go out nowhere. . . . They have literally no authority or influence in the house. They are very seldom admitted to the churches, and still less to friendly meetings."

Olearius, writing a century later (1643) noted that "the women are well proportioned; neither too big, nor too little; having passable good faces, but they paint so palpably, that if they laid it on with a brush, and had a handful of meal cast in their faces when they had done, they could not disfigure themselves as much as the paint does. But the custom is so general, that the most handsome must comply, lest they should discredit the artificial beauty of others; whereof we saw an example in the wife of Prince Borisovich Cherkassii, who was the handsomest lady in all of Muscovy, and was loath to spoil with painting what the rest of her sex took such pains to preserve thereby; but the other women informed against her, and would not be quiet, till their husbands had forced the prince to give way that his wife might daub her face in the ordinary manner. . . .

"Married women put up their hair within their caps or coifs, but the maids let theirs hang down the back in two tresses. . . . Children under ten years of age, as well girls as boys, have their hair cut, all except two moustaches, which are left over the temples; so that there being no difference in their habits, that of their sex is discovered only by the two brass or silver rings, which the girls wear in their ears."

Russia's scientific progress lagged far behind that of the rest of Europe. It was not until the beginning of the 18th Century, when Peter the Great made his enormous effort to drag his country into the modern world, that indigenous scientific talent began to make its impact felt. In part the lag resulted from the relentless opposition of the church to all secular studies—"The study of geometry," said one bishop, "is a spiritual sin." In part, too, it stemmed from Russian fear and suspicion of the West, and a consequent reluctance to accept foreign ideas.

For centuries Russia was split by a debate—which continues into our own time—between "Slavophiles" and "Westernizers." The Slavophiles held that Russia must develop her own pride, her own culture and her own institutions, and that she must find that unique place among nations, neither European nor Asiatic, that God had intended for her. Their opponents, the Westernizers, saw only backwardness and failure in Russia, and they ardently advocated the wholesale adoption of European ideas, techniques and values.

For practical reasons, largely military, both Ivan the Great and Ivan the Terrible were Westernizers to a degree. They imported metalworkers and other craftsmen from Europe. In 1652 Czar Alexis assigned the foreign workers a suburb in Moscow that was called the Nemetskaya Sloboda or "German Quarter." (With the exception of Swedes, Slavs and Latins, the Russians called all Europeans Germans, the Russian word for which is derived from the word for dumb.) From these foreign artisans the Russians learned various industrial skills—for example, how to cast cannon and church bells—and with the enthusiasm of the novice set out to surpass their teachers. In the 16th Century they cast an enormous bell, a monstrous object called "Czar Kolokol" which weighed almost 300,000 pounds, and a cannon named "Czar Pushka," which had a barrel nearly a yard wide. Unfortunately the bell was too large to be hung, and the cannon too broad to fire. The Russians became masters of these and other mechanical arts, while the Slavophiles in the background continually grumbled about Western influences.

In written literature also, Russia developed slowly—the first of her writers of world stature was Alexander Pushkin, who did not begin to produce his great work until the second quarter of the 19th Century. The Russian literary past was not entirely barren—the autobiography of the Archpriest Avvakum, quoted earlier, in Chapter 5, is much admired for its power and style, deriving much of its strength from the fact that Avvakum abandoned the restrictions and artificialities of Church Slavonic and wrote as he spoke, in the Russian vernacular. A few of the writers of the early chronicles, especially of the famous *Primary Chronicle*, also had undoubted literary gifts.

However, only one work of high genius is known to have been produced in all the years between the Christianization of Russia in the 10th Century and the 19th—*The Lay of Igor's Campaign*. This poem, which Pushkin called "that lonely monument in the desert of our literature," was composed by an unknown author at some time around the year 1200, and remained undiscovered until 1795, when a manuscript copy was found in Moscow.

The subject of the *Lay* is the campaign of Prince Igor against the Polovtsy of the steppe in 1185. At first victorious, then defeated and captured, Igor at length escapes and returns to his wife Yaroslavna. Written in a rhythmical prose, the *Lay* is neither a lyric nor an epic, but combines elements of both in a strikingly beautiful way. One of its finest passages—unhappily, the Russian rhythms dis-

appear in translation—is the lament of Igor's wife who, not knowing his fate, waits for him in the city of Putivl. The tone is reminiscent of that of an Old Testament psalm of David.

It is the voice of Yaroslavna which is heard.
Since morning she sings like an unknown seagull.
Like a seagull I will fly along the River Danube.
I will dip my beaver trimmed sleeve into the River Kaiala.
I will cleanse the bloody wounds of my prince,
on his mighty body.

O wind, why do you my lord wind,
blow so fiercely?
Why do you bring on your light wings
Kuman arrows against the warriors of my beloved?
Isn't it enough for you to blow under the clouds,
to loll the ships on the blue sea?
Why, my lord, did you scatter my joy
over the feathergrass of the prairie?

The most remarkable cultural achievements of Kievan and Muscovite Russia were the architecture and art—specifically in icon painting. During the years immediately following the conversion of Kiev to Christianity, masters from Byzantium supervised the construction and decoration of Russian churches, and as late as the 1470s Ivan III imported Italians to help build cathedrals in the Kremlin. However, native artisans were extensively employed on the construction of these works, and Russian taste obliged the foreigners to incorporate designs that would never have occurred to them in Byzantium or Venice.

Byzantine churches, for example, ordinarily had few domes—five might have been a maximum number, with the largest symbolizing Christ and the four others standing for the writers of the Gospels. In Russia, early churches frequently had 13 domes (which stood for Christ and the Twelve Apostles), and often many more. The typical "onion" shape of these domes, although it had antecedents in Islamic architecture, was the direct product of the hopeful simplicity of the Russian faith—the Heaven-aimed points of the domes, surmounted by crosses, were, to the devout Russian believer, signposts to salvation, intended to pierce the sky and not, like the round domes of the West, merely to repeat its curve.

In the north, where the skilled axman produced his utilitarian wonders, it was common in church architecture to make a very lofty, wedge-shaped or conical roof that would shed snow. A few northern churches, all of them made of wood, soared as high as 200 feet—an altitude that has prompted some critics to describe their architectural style as "Russian Gothic."

The Russian delight in churches is grimly evident in an anecdote concerning Ivan the Terrible. It is Ivan's church, St. Basil's Cathedral, that first impresses any visitor to the Red Square in Moscow. Ivan ordered its construction to commemorate his historic victory over the Tartars in Kazan. Multicolored and multi-domed, a tutti-frutti in paint and stone, St. Basil's still bewilders and enchants the Western eye, precisely as it enchanted Ivan's. It is said that the capricious Czar summoned the two luckless Russian architects who had designed the cathedral and, after offering them his congratulations, ordered their eyes to be dug out with knives, so that they might never again produce anything so beautiful.

Icon painting, inherited from Byzantium, assumed in Russian hands a wholly different character. Russians, with the Byzantines, strongly rejected naturalistic portraiture—who has seen the face of God? They also rejected perspective and three-dimensional modeling, for much the same reason. Still in their flat paintings they introduced a deep humanizing warmth, bringing a distant God closer to the understanding of a naive people. Of-

ten they accomplished this by the superb use of color. In Novgorod, for example, red was predominant (indeed, the Russian words for "red" and "beautiful" are synonyms); in the city of Tver, light blue was much used.

The great master of Russian icon painting, Andrei Rublev, who lived at the juncture of the 14th and 15th Centuries, had no contact with his Western contemporaries and so developed his style independently. The Russian critic Lazarev says this of Rublev: "He takes the colors for his palette not from the traditional canons of color, but from the Russian nature around him, the beauty of which he acutely sensed. His marvelous deep blue is suggested by the blue of the spring sky; his whites recalled the birches so dear to a Russian; his green is close to the color of unripe rye; his golden ochre summons up the color of autumn leaves . . . he translated the colors of Russian nature into the lofty language of art."

Icon painting was an important contribution by Russian artists to the culture of the world. Sculpture, in Russian hands, was not—Russians accepted the Byzantine view that representations of large human figures fall into the category of idolatry, as they produced only miniatures and bas-reliefs. In music, despite the fact that foreign visitors found the peasants constantly singing, the Russians had only a primitive style. However, it is the works of such 19th Century composers as Moussorgsky, Borodin, Rimsky-Korsakov and Tchaikovsky that old Russian music, long remembered, finds its best expression.

In any event, the Russian people did develop an indigenous culture—and they did so because of, and not in spite of, the crudity and vigor that so irritated the early foreign visitors. And the sources of this future artistic development were clearly visible in the nation even before the 16th Century—if the foreigners had only had the wisdom and the will to perceive them.

A GENTLEMAN'S SLEIGH *reflects the luxury enjoyed by the rich; such conveyances were often pulled by wretched-looking horses tended by ragged serfs.*

THROUGH ENGLISH EYES

In the 14th and 15th Centuries, most Europeans viewed Russia as a land of darkness; to journey into her interior, it was said, was to embark upon a fateful trip from which one might never return. In the 16th Century, when travelers actually penetrated this region, the tales they brought back were almost as strange as the legends that had sprung from ignorance. Russia, they reported, was a nation of extremes, with a bitter winter cold that changed abruptly into the balmy warmth of spring, with rich feudal estates that were filled with thousands of impoverished serfs, with a populace that offered foreigners bread and salt in token of friendship but remained deeply suspicious. Though most accounts were harshly critical, Russia continued to exert a powerful fascination over the rest of Europe. One of the most vivid reports was brought back by two Englishmen, John Atkinson and James Walker. Their account, written in the 18th Century, was augmented by Atkinson's illustrations, which offer a rich sampling of the things that intrigued, baffled—and occasionally delighted—visitors from abroad.

COLD AND COLORFUL MARKETS

Among the most amazing sights visitors saw in Russia were the open-air winter markets that were held in every major town—great outdoor refrigerators of milling people, sleds and huge mounds of frozen provisions. "Your astonished sight," wrote one Englishman, "is there arrested by a vast open square, containing the bodies of many thousand animals piled in pyramidical heaps on all sides. Cows, sheep, hogs, fowls, butter, eggs, fish are all stiffened into granite." These frozen provisions were brought on sleds from every corner of Russia. For foreigners it was a revelation that frozen foods could be thawed with almost no loss of flavor.

The markets reached a peak of activity just before Christmas, presenting a joyful social scene. Noblemen rubbed shoulders with serfs, merchants greeted old customers, peasants tearfully embraced lost friends and relatives. Many people came from far away, hoping to run into a man from their family who had been conscripted into the army and might now be stationed near the market town. "Nothing can be more affecting," recalled an Englishman, "than to witness their joyful meetings: fathers embracing their sons, brothers their brothers."

STOCKING UP ON FOOD, *holiday shoppers bargain over piles of frozen animals in St. Petersburg (left), while a housewife carts away her purchase in a small sled (foreground).*

A DRABLY DRESSED MERCHANT *wears the robelike caftan that identifies him. Most Russians wore caftans, but merchants wore unusually long ones, and dispensed with the usual sash.*

A GAILY BEDECKED WOMAN, *a merchant's wife, wears a brocaded smock that contrasts strongly with her husband's simple attire. Her tall headdress and long shawl signify that she is married.*

LOG HOUSES *of a small northern Russian village stand by the side of a rough, tree-lined road. At the left, a peasant woman uses a sweep to draw a bucket of water from a well.*

THE SIMPLE LIFE OF A VILLAGE

Sophisticated European travelers were astonished and repelled by the harsh life of the Russian villages. Such communities consisted of anywhere from a dozen to several hundred wooden houses clustered along a dirt or wooden street adjacent to a stream. In the north the village houses were made of logs insulated with moss; in the tree-scarce southern steppes they were generally made of clay and mud. A whole family lived, worked, ate and slept in a single room; often there was no chimney, and the smoke had to escape through shutters that covered the windows.

For entertainment the people visited one another, drank, and sang melancholy songs. Travelers were appalled by the amount of drinking that went on—especially when they had to join in. One Englishman warily commented that the Russians seemed to feel that getting drunk on holidays showed respect to the saints —and, he said, there were many holidays.

TILLING THE SOIL, *a peasant breaks the earth with a primitive plow. Partly because of such crude tools, most Russian fields produced low yields.*

HIGH SPIRITS *prevail among revelers at a local village tavern. The drinks usually sold were kvass (made of fermented bread), beer and wine.*

A PEASANT'S HOME *consisted of one room built around the fireplace. Here a girl puts the baby to sleep in a suspended cradle, while the boys lie down on pallets on top of the warm oven.*

A COUNCIL OF ELDERS *meets to discuss such village affairs as payment of local taxes, rents and the recruitment of soldiers. The oldest villager, who is leaning on his stick, presides.*

A RUSSIAN PEASANT *wears his summer attire: a deep-crowned hat, a white tunic that drapes over wide linen trousers and, around his legs, rags that are secured with pieces of twine.*

WASHING THE HORSES *after the day's work, peasants would either lead the beasts into a stream by long tethers or doff their clothes and ride the mounts into the cooling water.*

TAKING THE CROWN, which signifies both martyrdom and joy, an aristocratic young couple are joined in marriage. The lighted tapers held by the priest signified the hope for a happy marriage. Newlyweds usually went to live with the groom's family.

CONSECRATING THE WATERS, Church notables enter a temporary structure built on the Neva River in St. Petersburg to bless the water, as thousands watch. The ceremony, one of the major ones in Russian Orthodoxy, celebrated Christ's baptism.

A PIOUS, ROISTERING PEOPLE

The deep piety of the Russians impressed most visitors. Every home had its icon, and church attendance was unfailing. But many customs struck foreigners as peculiar; the English especially criticized the goings-on during religious holidays. The Russians, they objected, leavened their worship with gaiety, drinking and an interminable ringing of bells, but left out (as one visitor remarked) the things that Englishmen really wanted: "cushioned pews [and] silken hassocks to render piety pleasant."

BEARDED MONKS *converse animatedly near the entrance to a church, while a worshiper receives a priest's blessing. The triangular objects are wooden grave markers.*

DEVOUT PILGRIMS *pray before a wayside shrine. Often water was scarce and near a well would be a saint's image. After refreshing themselves, travelers offered devotions.*

WASHING CLOTHES, a Russian woman uses a wooden paddle to beat the soap and water out of her laundry, while a man with a long-handled dipper fills a wooden cask.

ICE CUTTERS load blocks onto a sled. Russians lined their cellars with these massive ice chunks, which formed a solid wall to preserve food during the summer months.

THE RIGORS OF WINTER

Foreigners never ceased to marvel at the Russians' ability to withstand the winter. As soon as the first snow fell, the people donned caps, furs, gloves and muffs, along with hobnail boots to keep from slipping on the ice. The wealthier householders installed storm windows, and lined doors and floors with felt. Holes were cut in the ice for drawing water, fishing and washing clothes.

But foreigners could never adjust to the cold; one Englishman commented, "You could cast water into the air and it would freeze before touching the ground." In January the country became a great frozen waste of snow, solitude and howling winds. Winter nights in the far north lasted almost 20 hours, and packs of starving wolves menaced lonely villages, attacking livestock and sometimes people. Houses contracting in the cold cracked in the dark with reports as loud as gunshots, and often travelers, an English ambassador said, were "brought into towns sitting dead and stiff in their sleds."

SEASONAL AMUSEMENTS

The Russian people, one British visitor observed, possessed a "national propensity to mirth," and they were never happier than at the turn of the seasons. The approach of spring was celebrated with an exuberant week-long carnival when every town set up rides and swings in the public square, and the populace gathered to watch traveling players, street dances and open-air boxing matches.

The beginning of winter created similar excitement. When the first snow fell, the Russians greeted it with great cheers. "They sing, they laugh, they wrestle," wrote an English painter, "tumbling about like great bears amongst the furrows of the surrounding snow." In the flat countryside the favorite winter diversion for peasants and aristocrats alike was sledding down steep artificial ice hills.

HAWKING BREAD, *a vendor strolls through a fair selling a tray of "ka-lachi." These twisted loaves, made of the finest flour, were a favorite of the people; they were eaten as snacks, alone or with a cup of coffee.*

WOODEN ICE HILLS *provided steep slopes for sledding. The person at the front of each sled was the passenger, the man behind steered. The more elaborate hills rose as high as 35 feet; the green boughs were decorations, intended simply to lend a festive air.*

AN EASTER CARNIVAL, *complete with whirling rides and strolling players, draws crowds in a Russian town. Such fêtes were often followed by tragedy: the celebrants got drunk and grew careless with fires; more than once an entire wooden town burned down.*

8

PETER THE GREAT

In the spring of the year 1697, traveling west, there came out of Russia a fantastic troop of men called "The Great Embassy." Among the swarm of Cossack outriders, drummers, trumpeters and prancing dwarfs there were a few richly robed grandees of apparently high rank—and one rough-clad man who said that his name was Peter Mikhailov and who pretended that he was of small account. This was Peter the Great, Czar of all Muscovy, who for reasons best known to himself did not want to be recognized. The idea was of course ludicrous: at 25, Peter stood nearly seven feet tall, and he had other characteristics well known by report in the West. He had a prominent wart on his shaven cheek; he suffered from a nervous ailment that frequently made his face twitch and his eyes roll; and his physique must have been remarkable: he was physically so powerful that he could take a heavy silver plate in his hands and roll it up like a scroll of parchment.

Passing through the Swedish-held Baltic port of Riga (the Swedes knew who he was, well enough, but did not acknowledge him), Peter and his retinue went next into Prussia. There, pretending that he was a simple "bombardier," he took lessons from a Prussian colonel of artillery. Whenever he saw pieces of mechanical equipment—clockwork, navigational instruments, complex contrivances of any kind—he wanted to know how they worked. As a rule he could guess their purpose at a glance, and could take them apart and reassemble them. All practical sciences, including anatomy, fascinated him. In the surgical theater of Boerhaave he observed a dissection, and for a moment dropped his pretense of meek obscurity. Noting that some members of his noble entourage were disgusted, he ordered them to advance upon the cadaver, bend over it and sever its nerves with their teeth. Peter was a cruel, often sadistic, man but almost invariably he was purposeful. In this grim instance he wished to drive home his point that Russia must learn about science from the West; if this required the members of his entourage to put aside their squeamishness, forget their ingrained dislike of things foreign and bury their faces in the bowels of a corpse, so be it.

In Holland, in the role of a common ship's car-

THE WESTERNIZER *who guided Russia into the modern world is shown in European military garb. This portrait of Peter was done in an especially developed glass mosaic technique by Michael Lomonosov, a noted scientist, writer and artist. It was completed in 1755, 30 years after Peter's death.*

BEARD LICENSES *showed that their bearers had paid a tax to remain unshaven. Peter imposed the tax in 1705 in his campaign to Westernize Russian fashion.*

penter, Peter labored furiously in a dockyard. In England he learned considerably more of shipbuilding. By now his disguise had slipped; the English acknowledged him as a great czar, and staged a mighty sham battle off Spithead for his benefit. They also found him a trifle boorish—Peter called on King William III in his shirtsleeves, and when he left the mansion that had been placed at his disposal near the shipyards of Deptford, it looked as if "Tartars had camped there." Doors had been ripped off their hinges, the grounds devastated and noble portraits riddled by musket balls. According to contemporary reports, Peter paid for the damage by handing his host a dirty piece of paper in which a huge uncut diamond was wrapped.

By way of Holland and Austria, Peter returned to Russia after a tour of 14 months, leaving behind him a gabble of amused or outraged conversation that did not subside for years. The Western Europeans did not—at that time—fear him, and many found his massive drinking bouts, his lechery and his seeming ignorance of the use of silverware laughable. However, not all observers were deceived by appearances. The great German philosopher Gottfried Leibniz held Peter in the highest regard, and others marveled with the Bishop of Burnet that "the providence of God . . . has raised up such a furious man to so absolute authority over so great a part of the world."

Who was this "furious man," the first Russian czar ever to visit Western Europe? He was a Romanov, to be sure, the son of Czar Alexis, and he had become sole sovereign of Russia at the age of 24 in 1696, after the death of his brother, and co-czar, Ivan. However, Peter was not in the gentle, ineffectual Romanov tradition; already he had far

outleaped the thoughts and attitudes of old Muscovy. During the 17th Century Western ideas had steadily been infiltrating the upper classes of Russia, and in the slow course of events another century might have passed before the infiltration began to have profound effects. Peter chose to hasten the process, to attempt to force his country into the Western world within his own lifetime and by the sheer power of his will.

As a boy and young man Peter shunned the Kremlin, spending much time in the German Quarter of Moscow. He despised ornate ceremonies and unreasoning tradition, much preferring the company of practical English, Scottish, Swiss and Danish technicians who could satisfy his enormous mechanical curiosity. At 12 he learned stonemasonry, and then carpentry. Ultimately he became expert in some 14 specialties, and with his huge, skilled hands he could shoe a horse, build a house, cast a cannon or pull a tooth. (He kept a small bagful of teeth as evidence of this talent.)

Peter enjoyed the company of these "Germans" not only because of their skills but also because of their Rabelaisian tastes, which precisely suited his own. At a very early age he learned to drink prodigiously, to smoke, to make love and to revel in coarse good humor and practical jokes, most of them of an unprintable nature. He also learned a principle that guided him throughout his life: advancement in any field, he concluded, should be based on merit and not on rank or origin. In later years he chose several of his assistants from the lowest levels of society, and at one time one of his regiments contained 300 young Russians who bore the title of prince—all of them serving as enlisted men. If they mastered their jobs, Peter would promote them; if they did not, they remained where they were.

When he was not studying or roistering among the foreigners, Peter passed his days in a village near Moscow, surrounded by young nobles, serfs, grooms and kennel boys. These he organized into regiments to stage mock battles and to build a large fort. Foreign officers, among them the fine Scottish General Sir Patrick Gordon, came out from Moscow to drill the "troops" and to give them advice on fortifications, and before long the young Czar began to requisition cannon, small arms and ammunition from the Kremlin arsenal. In one "sham" siege of the fort no fewer than 24 young men were killed—and, as General Gordon noted with some asperity, a five-pound rocket "took off the head of a boyar."

Of scholarly accomplishments Peter had almost none. He was literate, knew the mathematics required in military or naval affairs, and could make himself understood in Dutch, but in no other foreign language. Only toward the end of his life did he begin to think theoretically; before that he was concerned only with what was practical and of immediate use. However, these practicalities covered an immensely wide range—when he wished to improve the printing of Russian books, for example, he cut the type himself—and the quickness of his mind, his inexhaustible energy and his persistence were astonishing to all who came in contact with him. If he was not in fact a genius there seems no other word that adequately describes him.

Peter very early developed a clear sense of his mission as czar: to break the bonds of inflexible custom that had so long confined old Muscovy, with its shibboleth of "So it has been done from the time of our ancestors," and to lead his country "toward a new day, which shall be better than this." He believed this goal required the wholesale adoption of European technology and cultural attitudes—a conclusion strongly reinforced by what he saw during "The Great Embassy." Peter had only a superficial understanding of what Westernization actually entailed—he saw the achievements of England and Holland merely in their technical aspects, overlooking the centuries of culture that had made their development possible. Nor did he have the support of the Russian people for his plans; perhaps 95 percent of them actively or passively opposed him. Thus his accomplishments, limited or soon nullified though some of them were, seem all the more remarkable.

The history of Peter's reign is one of constant motion and commotion—only a single year of it passed without war, and during his entire adult life he is said never to have spent more than three months at a time in one place. His mind teemed with reforms and innovations; at one moment he would be concerned with agriculture (he was the first to import potatoes into Russia), and in the next with opening diplomatic relations with Madagascar. Perhaps the most convenient means of assessing Peter is to consider his career from two aspects, first in foreign and then in domestic policy.

Even before "The Great Embassy" Peter had set about to enlarge and strengthen his country by war. He wanted control of the southern steppe, then dominated by the last of the nomadic hordes, the Crimean Tartars; and he wanted access to the Black Sea, which was, in effect, the private lake of the Ottoman Turks. In 1695, at 23, he led an army south to besiege the fortress of Azov. (Actually he did not "lead" the army in person—his high commanders were foreign officers, including General Sir Patrick Gordon. Peter, practicing what he preached, served in the lowly post of gunner.) The attack failed—Azov was supplied by sea, and could not be forced to yield to assault by land.

Characteristically, Peter took his defeat only as a spur and a lesson. During the winter of 1695-1696,

at the city of Voronezh, 325 miles north of Azov on the Don, he built Russia's first navy in order to make a second attack. Ruthlessly impressing thousands of men into his service, and watching with detachment while they died of cold, disease, exhaustion and the knout, he constructed a fleet of seagoing vessels and transport barges, and with the coming of spring he returned to Azov. This time the fortress fell; and although its loss was not a serious blow to the Turks, Peter's success served notice to Europe that an uncommonly able man was rising in Russia.

During "The Great Embassy" Peter was widely congratulated on his victory, although he was unable to find European allies to help him in his battle with the infidels. (He did, however, secure some 35,000 muskets and the services of more than 700 technicians, in every specialty from medicine to mining, who took his pay and returned with him to Russia, the vanguard of thousands of artisans and professional men who later followed.)

In 1700, after arranging a truce with the Turks, Peter embarked upon the most important of all his military ventures—the Great Northern War. In alliance with Poland, Saxony and Denmark, he presumed to attack Sweden, a country then of great size (it included Finland and most of the Baltic coast), which, with France, maintained the balance of power in continental Europe. Peter's idea was similar to Ivan the Terrible's: to seize a "window" on the Baltic and transform his country into a sea power of the first rank.

The Great Northern War began with disaster. The 18-year-old King of Sweden, Charles XII, was thought to be a callow youngster who could easily be outmaneuvered—but in fact he turned out to be a military genius. At the Battle of Narva on the Baltic coast, although his forces were heavily outnumbered, he smashed the Russian army, killing or capturing 10,000 men and forcing 30,000 others to

run for their lives, abandoning all their artillery. At that point, in the opinion of most historians, Charles might easily have driven east to Moscow and put an end to the Russian threat. However, he in turn underestimated the Russians—Peter, in particular—and he broke off the Russian campaign to move south to deal with Poland, which he considered his major enemy. For six years he fought brilliantly but inconclusively there, allowing Peter more than enough time to recover.

In a frenzy of activity, Peter created a new and far larger army. Although the principle of mandatory state service by the nobility had long been established, Peter pushed it to the extreme. Noblemen were drafted no longer for a season or a campaign, but for life, as were peasant infantrymen. Church bells, the symbols of old Muscovy, were melted down to make cannon. New and more skilled foreign officers were imported, and the old military training manuals modernized. The bayonet, which theretofore had been regarded in Europe only as a defensive weapon, became in Russian hands a terrible means of attack. Peter himself took a wholly new approach to his function as czar. On one military order, which included the customary phrase "in the interests of his Czarist Majesty," he crossed out the words and substituted "in the interests of the State." Although he was indeed the most autocratic of all European monarchs, he regarded himself as the prime servant of the nation.

While Charles XII was embroiled in Poland, Peter was able to mount several small, successful campaigns on the Baltic. Above all, he seized the mouth of the river Neva, and in 1703 began to build a new capital named after himself: St. Petersburg (today, Leningrad). The site he chose was abominable—swampy, frequently inundated by tides, wretchedly cold and bleak. However, it was perfect for what Peter had in view in moving the capital: the shattering of Muscovite tradition and the advance into a new world. To build his city he dragooned into his service countless thousands of Russians—many of them from as far away as Astrakhan—paid them nothing, shrugged at their misery and death, and drove them onward. The great city today is perhaps less a tribute to his memory than to the heroic and unknown men who suffered and died to create it. Later he forced thousands of Russian noblemen, on pain of exile or execution, to move to St. Petersburg and build stone mansions there.

In part because of Peter's almost unbearable wartime taxation, and in part because of his ruthless drafting of men and his detested Western ideas, he found himself in 1705-1707 involved in wars with his own people. The struggle with Sweden was temporarily in abeyance, but in southern Russia the citizens of Astrakhan blazed with rebellion, and soon were joined by the Cossacks of the Don, led by Konrad Bulavin. The Old Believers, still opposed to Patriarch Nikon's 17th Century church reforms, were prominent in these revolts, which were suppressed only with the greatest difficulty. For a time it appeared that the whole of southern Russia might break away from the territory under Peter's control, and perhaps fall under the domination of the Turks. However, Peter's generals—who now included more Russians than foreigners—managed to defeat Bulavin in 1708, and to secure Peter's flank for the oncoming confrontation with Charles XII.

The Swedish King, weary of his struggle in Poland, chose to spend the winters of 1708-1709 in the Ukraine, where he hoped to rest his troops, secure aid from the Zaporogian Cossacks, and later advance on Moscow. However, the Cossacks failed to supply the help they had promised, and in July, 1709, a badly supplied Swedish army of about 25,000 came face to face with 40,000 Russians at Poltava, southeast of Kiev. On this occasion Peter led his troops himself, and won a battle that has been ranked among the 20 most important military engagements in world history.

Only a few of the Swedes at Poltava escaped death or capture, among them Charles XII, who fled south and found asylum in Turkey. The great victory might well have marked the end of Peter's military career, but, as matters developed, it was merely the midpoint. France, deeply alarmed at the emergence of Russian power, incited Turkey to declare war on Peter in 1710, and in the following year the Czar led his army south to meet the challenge. Doubtless Peter was overconfident because of his success against the Swedes, and certainly he counted heavily (and foolishly) on the support of Orthodox Christians in the Turkish principalities of Wallachia, Moldavia, Serbia and Montenegro. In any event, on the river Pruth, not far from its juncture with the Danube near the Black Sea, Peter was surrounded by an enormous Turkish force and was obliged to surrender. For reasons that have never been made clear, the Turks did not annihilate him but let him off on surprisingly easy terms. Peter surrendered Azov and gave up his Black Sea fleet, while the refugee king, Charles XII, went safely home to Sweden.

The indomitable Charles immediately renewed the Great Northern War, and the Swedes were able to continue it for 10 years, though with increasingly heavy losses. The Czar, in his new capital at St. Petersburg and the nearby fortress and shipyard at Kronstadt, constructed a truly formidable, modern fleet—indeed, the English were so distressed by it that in 1719 they summarily withdrew all their naval personnel from Peter's service and began to speak of him as a menace to world peace. As admiral, Peter defeated a Swedish squadron at the battle of Hangö, and then, as general, invaded Finland and finally Sweden itself. In 1721 the war was over, and in the peace treaty Sweden ceded to Russia substantially the territory now occupied by the Soviet Socialist Republics of Latvia and Estonia.

During the victory celebrations Peter accepted the title "emperor" and the epithet "the Great." Europe was slow to accept the notion of a Russian Emperor, having but lately considered Peter an oaf or an "Oriental despot," but by 1745, 20 years after Peter's death, even France acknowledged the title. There was no alternative. By his creation of an army and a navy and by his victories, Peter had placed his country militarily, if not culturally, among the great nations of Europe. In the future no alliance, no balance of power, could reckon without her.

Peter's domestic reforms and innovations were often connected with his military needs; some historians take the view that all of his Westernizing served only to advance his purposes in war. However, Peter's colossal goal involved not merely the building of fleets and armies and the raising of money to support them. He envisioned fundamental changes in all of Russian life—in government, society, industry and culture—and doubtless would have undertaken his reforms whether he had had a military goal or not.

For example, immediately upon his return from "The Great Embassy" he personally cut off the beards of several Muscovite nobles. This famous act was regarded by traditionalists and Old Believers as the blackest blasphemy—if man is created in the image of God, is not shaving an indirect mutilation of God? Peter also ordered the nobility and the men of the army and navy to dress in the Western style, "to sever the people from their former Asiatic customs and instruct them how all Christian people in Europe comport themselves." Such changes had no military application; they merely symbolized Peter's intention of transforming Muscovy into a modern Russia.

The administrative mechanism inherited by Peter was chaotically inefficient. All power was centralized in Moscow, in the person of the czar and in a mass of bureaus, which in confused and overlapping fashion dealt with police matters, law, mines, the fur trade, foreign relations and dozens of other state affairs. In the hope of establishing order, and desperate for money that could be collected only by a well-ordered government, Peter turned to Europe for ideas. He did not blindly imitate the West; he adapted its institutions to fit Russian circumstances.

Following the Swedish pattern, Peter decentralized his government, dividing his realm at first into eight, and ultimately into 50, provinces. Some improvement resulted, chiefly because it was no longer necessary to refer every petty problem to Moscow for decision, but the 50-province plan proved a failure. Peter counted on the local gentry to provide at least minimum leadership, and they were unable to do so.

To replace the defunct *Zemsky Sobor* and the boyar duma, Peter in 1711 created a nine-man senate to supervise all of the administrative, judicial

С АН КТ Ъ П І Т Е Р Б У Р Х Ъ,

В Ѣ Д О М О С Т И.

Изъ БЕРЛІНА 16 Октября.

Въ прошлои Вторнікъ Король Велі-
кобрітанскіи, простілся въ Шарло-
тенбургѣ съ Королевою Прускою,
и со всею Королевскою Фаміліею,
съ велікіми доказателствы усердія
и дружбы. На завтрѣѣ его Велічест-
ство, поѣхалъ отъ толь съ Королемъ
14   Прускімъ

RUSSIA'S FIRST NEWSPAPER *was founded in 1703 by Peter the Great, who wanted his people to know what was going on in the world. This issue reports meetings between the British and the Prussian Royal Family, under the headline "The News. From Berlin 16 October." The picture is thought to show St. Petersburg.*

and financial affairs of the state, and in 1717 he established a system of "colleges," which supplanted the thicket of government bureaus, and in the process relieved the overworked senate of some of its multitudinous duties.

The collegiate system was recommended to Peter by the philosopher Leibniz, who was retained by the Czar as an adviser and who frequently corresponded with him. There were originally nine colleges, replacing some 40 old Muscovite bureaus. Each college contained a dozen men, including at least one well-educated foreigner, and far from finding the system cumbrous, Peter thought it excellent. There was less chance of domination by one man, and hence of corruption; several heads, being wiser than one, would be less likely to produce foolish or arbitrary decisions. And in fact the colleges, which dealt with war, justice, taxation, foreign affairs, finance and economic development, for a time performed better than the bureaus they replaced.

Peter also "reformed" the Church, although there were many clergymen who did not find that an appropriate word. When the Patriarch Hadrian died in 1700, Peter deliberately neglected to appoint a successor and 21 years later emerged with the idea of a Holy Synod. There would no longer be a Patriarch in Russia; a committee of 10 clerics, supervised by a layman, would assume the patriarchal functions. In the future, the state would control Church organization, policies and possessions. The Holy Synod remained in operation until 1917, always subservient to the czar, and never able to challenge his authority.

In matters of finance, Peter's methods were at once ruthless and enlightened. In order to extract the last possible kopeck to pay for his wars, he placed taxes on coffins, on beehives, beards, bathhouses and all else that seemed remotely likely to yield revenue. His most far-reaching "reform" in

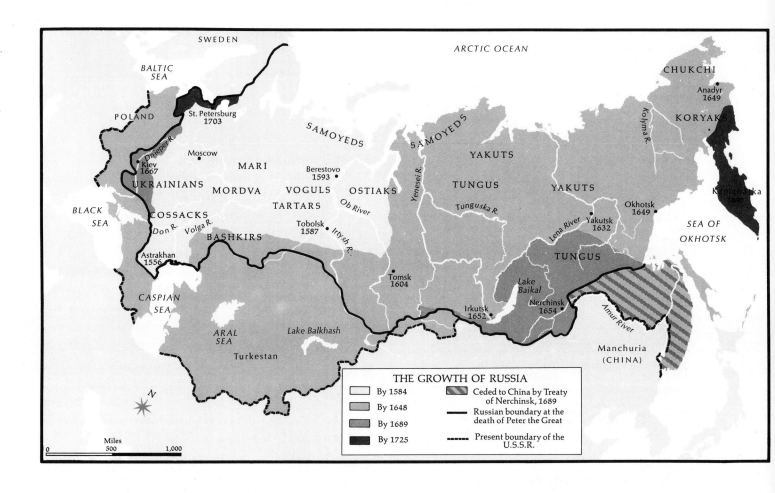

THE GROWTH OF RUSSIA

By 1584
By 1648
By 1689
By 1725

Ceded to China by Treaty of Nerchinsk, 1689
Russian boundary at the death of Peter the Great
Present boundary of the U.S.S.R.

the tax structure involved the introduction of a "soul" tax to replace the old levy on households —serfs and peasants, he found, had been evading the household tax by huddling together in large numbers under one roof. In 1718 Peter began a national census of all males of whatever age or condition; it required six years of bloody inquisition, conducted by the army, to root out and register all who were taxable. Ultimately more than five million males were inscribed, their souls reduced to the level of insensate commodities in the eyes of the government.

Meanwhile Peter made great efforts to create and nourish Russian industries. During his reign scores of manufacturing establishments were built at government expense, and still more were created by private individuals who received special concessions from the Czar. It was Peter who began the exploitation of the great copper and iron deposits in the Urals, developed a textile industry and promoted the manufacture of glass and leather.

As he struggled to modernize his country, Peter restlessly probed into every detail of the lives of his people. He abolished the custom of keeping women in seclusion; in the future, he commanded, men and women were to mingle freely at "assemblies" in private homes. To this order he added several paragraphs of instructions as to how host and guests should behave. He concerned himself with the smallest aspects of personal appearance, issuing a flood of edicts on the tailoring and color of clothing. He ordained the design of peasant houses, specifying that stoves should be placed on foundations, not on the floor, and that inflammable ceilings should be finished with clay and not left with beams exposed. "Caring for his subjects as a father," he promulgated assorted rules for maintaining physical fitness—and in case these should fail, he even specified the kind of gravestones that were to be erected.

In all his reforms Peter functioned as an enlightened despot; in his view, "the general good" required that the individual should be subordinate to the state. His innumerable edicts carried threats of dire punishment for those who disobeyed them, "for you know yourself that, though a thing be good and necessary, our people will not do it unless forced to." However, Peter did not rely solely on coercion; many of his laws contained appeals to reason, by which he hoped to educate his ignorant and tradition-bound subjects. In enjoining the people from allowing cattle and hogs to run loose in the streets of St. Petersburg, he noted that "such cattle deface roads and spoil trees." Forbidding the riding of unbridled horses, he explained that "this leads to much harm to people, for an unbridled horse cannot be quickly curbed."

In his zeal for education, Peter sent hundreds of young Russians to study abroad and founded many schools in his own country. The first of these emphasized the teaching of subjects useful in war, such as arithmetic, geometry, geography and navigation, but later dozens of elementary schools were established in the provinces. He also founded two medical schools, a public library and a museum, and at the time of his death was completing plans for his greatest cultural undertaking, the Imperial Academy of Science—in effect a university, with colleges of mathematics, history and physics.

When the first newspaper appeared in Russia, Peter himself edited it. He reformed the alphabet, replaced the awkward Slavic numerals with Arabic numbers, sponsored the printing of at least 600 different books, and reformed the Russian calendar to conform with the European—accomplishing all of this while he was engaged in war, and in the face of fanatical opposition from his people. The character of this opposition may be summed up in the reaction to his calendar reform. Russians, until Peter's time, numbered the years according to the Biblical account of the creation, and each new year began in September rather than in January. When Peter decreed his reform, the Old Believers and others advanced a maddening (though, from this distance, delightful) argument. The first year, they said, *must* have begun in September, when apples are ripe. Otherwise, how could the serpent have tempted Eve? What fruit could the serpent have found, on the bare boughs of January, to bring about the fall of man? Calendar reform was obviously the work of Antichrist—none other than Peter himself.

A balanced view of Peter demands that he be shown as something less than a white knight valiantly battling foreign foes and domestic ignorance. Although he never lapsed into the paranoia that seized Ivan the Terrible, he was fully as cruel. As a mild reproof to those who annoyed him, he would knock them senseless with his huge fist. When he was somewhat angrier, he would have iron pincers inserted into the noses of those who had offended him and their nostrils would be torn out. The number of men tortured and executed at Peter's command is beyond reckoning.

At 17 Peter married a girl of aristocratic family, Eudoxia Lopukhina, who bore him a son, Alexis. However, Peter soon tired of her old-Russian ways and apparent narrowness of mind, and in 1698 forced her into a nunnery. He never established a close relationship with his son, who took no interest in Peter's reforms and in fact refused to endorse them. When the young man was 29, Peter became convinced that Alexis was involved in a plot against him. After severe "questioning," which involved the knout, Alexis died in prison. Peter appeared quite unmoved; his son's body was scarcely cold before the Czar hurried off to watch the launching of a new ship that he had designed. By that time Peter had other children, born to a Lithuanian woman named Catherine who was of peasant origin and with whom he had been living happily for several years. In 1712 he married Catherine, and later gave her the title of Empress. The marriage of Catherine and Peter was a happy one. She was an energetic woman and so devoted to her husband that she traveled with him wherever he went, even on military campaigns.

In view of Peter's violent mode of life, it is surprising that he survived as long as he did. Throughout his life he suffered from some unidentified affliction that displayed itself in facial twitches and occasional convulsions. By middle age he was probably an alcoholic, and he had a fearfully painful condition diagnosed as "strangury and stone," apparently involving his kidneys and bladder. In February, 1725, when he was 53, Peter the Great died; soon thereafter his former subjects rejoiced in repeating the caption of a famous cartoon: "The Mice Bury the Cat."

The accomplishments and legacy of Peter the Great have been endlessly debated; the man was so many-sided that both the Russian liberal intellectuals of the 19th Century and the Stalinists of the 20th Century saw their progenitor in him. Some historians regard Peter as a revolutionary; others hold that this was not at all the case—that Peter demanded a new way of life for Russia, not a new form of government. In the eyes of the Slavophiles, Peter betrayed his heritage and his country; to the Westernizers he is an incomparable hero. Reckless, thoughtful, tyrannical, benevolent, boorish, charming, brilliant, shallow-minded—all these adjectives have been applied to him at one time or another, and all with some justice.

More than two centuries after his death, the definitive biography of Peter remains to be written. There is general agreement about the man only in certain areas: he was a great patriot, and all that he did was done in what he conceived to be the interests of his beloved country. Peter was not the first to glimpse Russia's destiny. No doubt Grand Prince Vladimir of Kiev, who welcomed the Cross and the culture of Byzantium so long ago, had visions of it. So too had Alexander Nevsky, Ivan the Terrible and Boris Godunov, however dim and clouded the vision was, and however these great men were borne down by fate and circumstance. But it was Peter the Great who, at long last, succeeded in transforming the nation of Russia into a great world power and in linking it irrevocably with the West.

When Peter was sealed in his huge coffin, the centuries of Russian isolation were forever at an end; the power and the glory of old Muscovy were dead and the era of imperial Russia had begun. By 1725 the Russian national character had been molded. The national destiny had been to a great extent determined by the forces that had made Russian history, from the days of ancient Kiev to the days of St. Petersburg.

Ahead lay two and a half centuries of cultural triumph and political trial. The groundwork had been laid for the emergence of such cultural giants as the writers Alexander Pushkin, Nikolai Gogol, Ivan Turgenev, Fedor Dostoevsky, Leo Tolstoy and Anton Chekhov; the composers Alexander Borodin, Modest Moussorgsky, Nikolai Rimsky-Korsakov, Peter Tschaikovsky and Igor Stravinsky. It might even be said that with the encouragement of a new hope and ambition, the foundations had been laid for Russia's brilliant military and scientific accomplishments.

But the way had been prepared as well for the cruel repressions of the 19th Century, which led to the upheavals of the 20th. The Soviet Union, no less than imperial Russia—from Peter to Nicholas —is the child of early Russia, and its people are essentially the same as those of centuries ago: suspicious, cruel, brave, patient and kind. Viewed against the background of the triumphs and tragedies of Russia's past, the paradoxes of modern Russia seem more understandable.

IVAN'S BELL TOWER, *the Kremlin's tallest structure, rises above other gilded domes as a Moscow landmark.*

HALLS OF THE CZARS

To the Russian people the Kremlin represented the heart and history of their nation. Rising within a 64-acre compound at the center of Moscow, this home of Russia's czars and patriarchs was built of disparate elements—as was the nation—forever changing, yet somehow remaining as immutable as Russia itself. So much, in fact, did the Kremlin symbolize the old Russia that when Peter the Great decided to modernize the nation he abandoned the ancient, onion-domed enclave and started afresh with a whole new capital, St. Petersburg, 400 miles to the northwest.

AN ELEMENTAL STRENGTH IN STONE

As Moscow's power grew, so did the Kremlin. First erected as a flimsy pine stockade in the 12th Century, it attained greater permanence in the 14th Century when Prince Ivan Kalita—who made Moscow Russia's seat of power through clever dealings with the Mongol overlords—replaced its pine with massive walls of oak and built its first stone churches. Within two generations, Dimitry Donskoy, the first Russian prince to defeat the Mongols, rebuilt the walls of white sandstone, and the Kremlin began to take on the brooding sense of peasant strength that characterizes it to this day.

SOARING COLUMNS, *girdled with images of saints, support the dome of the Assumption Cathedral and its fresco of Christ.*

TESTAMENTS TO PIETY

Throughout the invasions and princely rivalries that tore Russia, the Church and the faith it propagated kept the people together. As testaments to this fierce piety, more than a dozen churches stood within the Kremlin walls. The most important was the Cathedral of the Assumption, erected in 1326 and rebuilt in 1479. Here, in Russia's equivalent of Westminster Abbey, czars were crowned and patriarchs and metropolitans were buried; here, among tiers of iconed saints and angels, light blazed from precious stones onto pillars overlaid with gold. The first boyars and bishops to stand amidst this medieval magnificence exclaimed: "We see heaven!"

AN ORNATE PORTAL, *painted blue and gold, opens onto the nave of the Cathedral of the Annunciation, the czars' own private chapel.*

TIERS OF ICONS, *lit by chandeliers, rise above a floor of jasper and agate in the Annunciation Cathedral, scene of royal weddings and christenings.*

A GARDEN OF DOMES *crowns the ornate Cathedral of St. Basil—*
actually nine separate churches, connected by vaulted passages.

A DECORATIVE STAIRWAY *of stone, gorgeously painted, leads*
to the czars' fourth-floor living quarters in the Terem Palace.

A FILIGREED CHAMBER, *in the Terem, where boyars awaited the*
Czar, was heated by a tile stove embellished with native designs.

A FLOWERING OF NATIVE STYLE

Surging in from the steppes and forests, the exuberant indigenous art of the Russian people, which was loved and fostered by native rulers, became an integral part of the palaces and the churches of the Kremlin. The Russian skill with floral forms, combined with the more sophisticated styles of the Western architects employed by the czars, contributed a bizarre delicacy and gaiety to what might otherwise have been massively tasteless opulence.

Some of the results were surprising indeed. St. Basil's Cathedral, just outside the Kremlin, struck a note of fantastic, jubilant beauty with its nine soaring, bulbous domes, each unique in color and design. Both the interior and the exterior of the Terem Palace, the official residence of the czars, were decorated with native motifs. These could transform even such a utilitarian object as a stove *(below)* into an imaginative piece of popular art.

WATER-SPOUTING NYMPHS, *in a grouping of Western neoclassical statues, adorn the Grand Cascade before Peter's palace, Peterhof.*

AN OLD MAN ON A DOLPHIN *symbolized the Volkhov River, a trade route linked to the Baltic Sea by Peter's victory over the Swedes.*

A FOUNT OF NEW IDEAS

As the old Kremlin symbolized Russian unification, the new capital of St. Petersburg reflected Peter the Great's determination to open Russia to the West. On a broad marsh close to his western frontier, Peter in 1703 set about building a European city with the help of an Italian architect, conscripted Russian laborers and his own demonic energy. To finance his project Peter imposed brutal taxes; to get building materials he ordered that everyone entering the city bring a building stone.

No 18th Century city grew so quickly, or at such cost. Transforming the pestilential marsh cost the lives of some 200,000 laborers, who died from fever and exposure. But within a decade Peter had his wish. In 1712 St. Petersburg was proclaimed capital of Russia and so it remained for 206 years, forever affecting the course of Russian history.

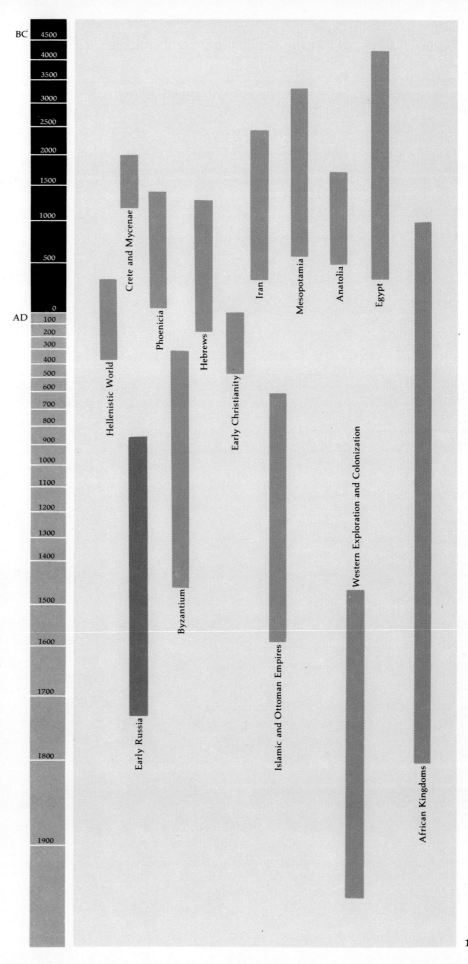

CROSSROAD CIVILIZATIONS BETWEEN EAST AND WEST

The chart at right is designed to show the duration of the early Russian period, and to relate it to those of others in the "Crossroad" group of cultures that are considered in one major series of volumes of this library. This chart is excerpted from a comprehensive world chronology that appears in the introductory booklet of the series. Comparison of the chart seen here with the world chronology will enable the reader to relate the rise of Russia to important cultural periods in other parts of the world.

On the following pages is a chronological listing of important events that took place in the period covered by this book.

CHRONOLOGY: *A listing of significant events during the Rise of Russia*

KIEVAN PERIOD

550	Slavs ("Sclaveni") are first mentioned by a Greek chronicler
862	Rurik arrives in Novgorod from Scandinavia and founds the Varangian Dynasty
879	Oleg, kinsman of Rurik, becomes ruler of Novgorod and later of Kiev, the "Mother of Russian Cities"
888-898	Cyril and Methodius, two monks sent from Constantinople as missionaries to the Slavs, develop the first written Slavic alphabet
907	Oleg and the Russes attack Constantinople and force formal trade treaties with the Byzantine Emperor
913	Igor succeeds Oleg as ruler of Kiev
945	Igor is killed on an expedition against the Drevlianians
946	Igor's wife Olga, ruling as regent, avenges Igor's death by burning the Drevlianian city and burying their ambassadors alive
955	Olga travels to Constantinople and is baptized, becoming the first prominent Russian Christian
972	Svyatoslav, Olga's son and Grand Prince of Kiev, is killed by the Pechenegs and his sons fight for supremacy
978	VLADIMIR becomes sole ruler of the Kievan realm
988	Vladimir sends emissaries to various Churches, chooses Eastern Orthodoxy for Russia and imposes Christianity on his subjects
996	The Church of the Tithe, first stone church in Russia, is completed
1015	Death of Vladimir is followed by 21 years of fratricidal strife, during which Svyatopolk murders his brothers Boris and Gleb
1025	The Monastery of the Caves is founded near Novgorod
1036	YAROSLAV "THE WISE" becomes Grand Prince of Kiev, beginning the golden age of the Kievan realm
	Russkaya Pravda, the first Russian code of laws, is written
1037	In Kiev, Yaroslav builds St. Sophia, modeled after its namesake in Constantinople, and the Church of the Annunciation
1054	Death of Yaroslav is followed by dissension and fighting among various Russian princes
1074	Death of Theodosius, abbot of the Monastery of the Caves
1113	VLADIMIR MONOMAKH becomes Grand Prince of Kiev and temporarily reunites the realm
1116	The monk Sylvester compiles *The Primary Chronicle*
1125	Death of Vladimir Monomakh marks the beginning of Kiev's decline
1147	First mention of Moscow in the Russian chronicles
1169	Andrei Bogolyubsky sacks and destroys Kiev
1185	*The Lay of Igor's Campaign*, an epic poem, marks the highpoint of Russian literature to this time

MONGOL PERIOD

1206	Temuchin unites all Mongol tribes and takes the name Genghis Khan
1223	Mongols destroy the Polovtsy-Russian army at the Battle of the river Kalka
1227	Genghis Khan dies; his heirs begin their "conquest of the world"
1237-1240	Batu Khan leads the Mongol invasion and conquest of Russia

1240	ALEXANDER, Prince of Novgorod, crushes the Swedes at the mouth of the Neva, winning the name "of the Neva" or Nevsky
1242	Alexander Nevsky defeats the Teutonic Knights at Lake Peipus
1252	Mongols name Alexander Nevsky Grand Prince of Russia
1263	Alexander Nevsky dies and leaves the principality of Moscow to Daniel, his youngest son
1316	Gedemin, King of the Lithuanian state, tries to gain control of Russia
1328	IVAN KALITA becomes Grand Prince of Moscow and sets the city on the road to supremacy in Russia
	The seat of the Orthodox Church is moved to Moscow from Vladimir
1340	Sergius of Radonezh founds the Holy Trinity Monastery near Moscow
1380	DIMITRY DONSKOY defeats the Mongols at the Battle of Kulikovo Pole
1386	Yagiello, ruler of Lithuania, marries Yadwiga of Poland, joining the two kingdoms in the fight against Russia
1392	Death of Sergius of Radonezh, who is later canonized as the patron saint of Muscovite Russia
1395	Tamerlane attacks the principality of Riazan, close to Moscow, but mysteriously turns back
1411	Andrei Rublev, Russia's greatest icon painter, completes his "Trinity"
1430	Khanate of the Crimea breaks away from the Mongol Empire
1438	Mongol Empire fragments into the khanates of Astrakhan, Kazan and Sibir
1438-1439	Council of Florence attempts to heal the breach between Eastern and Western branches of the Christian Church
1444	First mention of the Cossacks ("kozaks") in Russian chronicles
1453	Fall of Constantinople to the Turks leaves Russia as the bastion of Orthodoxy

MUSCOVITE PERIOD

1462	IVAN III "THE GREAT" becomes Grand Prince of Moscow and "Czar and Autocrat," and begins "The Gathering of the Russian lands"
1472	Ivan marries Sophia Paleologus, niece of the last Emperor of Byzantium, brings Italian architects and artisans to Russia, and adopts the Byzantine double-headed eagle as the symbol of Russian rulers
1470-1478	Ivan conquers and annexes the city-state of Novgorod, ending its 500 years of independence
1475-1479	The Cathedral of the Assumption is built in Moscow to the designs of the Italian architect Fiorvanti
1480	Russians force retreat of the Mongols at the Ugra River, ending formal Mongol domination of Russia; no more tribute is paid but Tartar khanates continue to harass Russia until 1783
1484-1489	Moscow's Cathedral of the Annunciation is built
1487-1491	The Palace of Facets, first great palace of the Kremlin, is constructed
1499	The Kremlin's Terem Palace is begun as the residence of the czar
1503	A Church council decides Russia's first great religious dispute by declaring for the "Possessors" over the "Non-Possessors"
1505-1509	Moscow's Cathedral of the Archangel Michael is built to designs by Alesio Nov, a Milanese architect, and later becomes the burial place of the czars
1505	On the death of Ivan the Great, Vasily III becomes ruler of Russia

1517	Count Sigismund Herberstein, Ambassador of the Holy Roman Emperor, visits Russia and brings back the first Western accounts
1533	IVAN IV "THE TERRIBLE" becomes czar at the age of three
1547	Ivan is officially crowned and marries Anastasia Romanov
1550	The first *Zemsky Sobor*, or national assembly, is called by Ivan to advise him
1552	Ivan defeats the Kazan Tartars and commands the building of St. Basil's Cathedral to commemorate the event
1553	Expedition of the Englishmen Willoughby and Chancellor opens trade routes to Russia
1556	Ivan conquers the Astrakhan Tartars
1558	The Livonian Wars begin
1560	Anastasia Romanov dies, setting Ivan on the road to madness
1560-1570	Moscow is proclaimed the "Third Rome" as the heir of Byzantium and the seat of the true Orthodox Church
1563	The first printing press is brought to Moscow by order of Ivan
1565	Ivan creates the *oprichnina*, a state within a state, and an eight-year reign of terror begins
1569	The Union of Lublin creates a dual state of Lithuania and Poland under one king, posing a continuing threat to Muscovy
1570	Suspecting treason, Ivan the Terrible destroys Novgorod, killing and torturing many thousands of its inhabitants
1571	The Crimean Tartars burn Moscow to the ground, leaving some 200,000 dead and taking at least 100,000 prisoners
1581-1583	Ermak Timofeevich, a Cossack, sets off on his expedition to Siberia, conquers the Khan of Sibir and adds Western Siberia to Muscovy
1583	Armistice with Poland and Sweden finally ends the 25-year Livonian Wars
1584	Ivan the Terrible dies and is succeeded by his feeble son Fedor, the last of the Varangian line, with Boris Godunov as regent
1588	English Ambassador Giles Fletcher presents his report on Russia to Queen Elizabeth
1589	First Russian Patriarch of the Orthodox Church, Metropolitan Job of Moscow, is appointed
1591	Young Prince Dimitry dies mysteriously
1598	BORIS GODUNOV, on Fedor's death, is elected czar by the Zemsky Sobor; the 15-year "Time of Troubles" begins
1601-1603	A great famine occurs in Russia, killing millions
1604	"False Dimitry," with the help of a Polish army, invades the Ukraine
1605	The death of Boris Godunov is followed by the enthronement of "False Dimitry"
1606	"False Dimitry" is killed by Russian boyars, his remains are burned and his ashes fired out of a cannon toward Poland
1610	Poles occupy and burn Moscow and new pretenders to the throne appear
1612	Kuzma Minin, a butcher, and Prince Pozharsky, a nobleman, re-take Moscow from the Poles
1613	MICHAEL ROMANOV is elected czar by the Zemsky Sobor; the "Time of Troubles" ends
1645	ALEXIS becomes czar at the age of 16 on the death of Michael Romanov
1648	Riots take place in Moscow over the salt tax
	In the Ukraine, Bogdan Khmelnitsky leads his Cossacks against Poland
	Russians reach the Pacific Ocean in their colonization of Siberia

1649	The *Ulozhenie*, or Code of Laws, establishes levels of Russian society, and in effect establishes serfdom by making it illegal for a peasant to leave the land
1652	Alexis establishes the German Suburb for foreigners in Moscow

PETRINE PERIOD

1653	Nikon becomes Patriarch of Moscow; his drastic reforms result in the schism of the "Old Believers"
	Bogdan Khmelnitsky and Zaporogian Cossacks swear allegiance to Alexis; war with Poland breaks out again
1667	Treaty of Andrusovo partitions the Ukraine between Russia and Poland
1670-1671	Stenka Razin, a Don Cossack, leads a great peasant revolt that is crushed by the Czar
1672	PETER THE GREAT, Czar Alexis' 14th child, is born to Natalia Naryshkin, the czar's second wife
1682	Peter becomes czar at the age of 10, but his half-sister Sophie engineers a palace revolt and becomes regent, making Peter co-czar with his half-brother Ivan
1682-1689	Sophie governs Russia as Peter spends his time playing soldier, or frequenting the German Suburb of Moscow
1689	Peter deposes Sophie and marries his first wife, Eudoxia Lopukhina
1696	On the death of Ivan, Peter becomes sole czar, defeats the Turks at Azov with the help of his new navy
1697	Peter starts his "Grand Embassy" to Europe, visiting Sweden, Prussia, Holland and England
1698	Revolt of the *Streltsy* causes Peter's return and execution of 1,700 rebels; Peter begins his campaign to Westernize Russian life
	Peter adopts the Julian calendar for Russia
1700	The Great Northern War with Charles XII of Sweden begins
1701	Russia's first School of Mathematics and Navigation is established by Peter
1703	By making a cross on the ground, Peter commences the building of St. Petersburg
	Russia's first newspaper, edited by Peter, and its first textbooks are printed
1708	The nobility is commanded to move from Moscow to St. Petersburg
1709	At the Battle of Poltava, Peter is victorious over Charles XII
1712	Peter marries his second wife, Catherine, a former peasant
	St. Petersburg is declared the official capital of Russia
1715	Alexandre Leblond, a French architect, is ordered to make designs for a new palace to rival Versailles; Peterhof is started
1719	Peter, suspecting his son Alexis of plotting against him, has him tortured to death
1721	Final victory over the Swedes ends the Great Northern War
1722	The Table of Ranks, ordered by Peter, becomes the foundation of Russian bureaucracy
1724	Peter's wife is crowned Catherine I
1725	Vitus Bering, a Danish explorer, is sent by Peter to find a new route to America through Siberia
	Peter dies, leaving the question of his succession unresolved

BIBLIOGRAPHY

These books were selected during the preparation of this volume for their interest and authority, and for their usefulness to readers seeking additional information on specific points.

An asterisk (*) marks works available in both hard-cover and paperback editions; a dagger (†) indicates availability only in paperback.

GENERAL HISTORY

Blum, Jerome, *Lord and Peasant in Russia.* Princeton University Press, 1961.
Carmichael, Joel, *An Illustrated History of Russia.* Reynal & Co., 1960.
Clarkson, Jesse, *A History of Russia.* Random House, 1963.
Cross, Samuel H., *Slavic Civilization Through the Ages.* Russell & Russell, 1963.
Dvornik, Francis, *The Slavs in European History and Civilization.* Rutgers University Press, 1962.
Fennell, John L.I., *Ivan the Great of Moscow.* St. Martin's Press, 1962.
Grekov, B., *Kiev Rus.* Moscow, Foreign Languages Publishing House, 1959.
Guershoon, Andrew, *Certain Aspects of Russian Proverbs.* London, Frederick Muller Ltd., 1941.
Hindus, Maurice, *The Cossacks.* Country Life Press, 1945.
Hrushevsky, Michael, *A History of the Ukraine.* Yale University Press, 1941.
Kerner, Robert J., *The Urge to the Sea.* University of California Press, 1946.
Kluchevsky, V.O., *A History of Russia.* Transl. by C.J. Hogarth. 5 vols. Russell & Russell, 1960.
*Kluchevsky, V.O., *Peter the Great.* Transl. by Liliana Archibald. St. Martin's Press, 1959.
*Kochan, Lionel, *The Making of Modern Russia.* London, Jonathan Cape, 1962.
Koslow, Jules, *The Kremlin.* Thomas Nelson & Sons, 1958.
Lamb, Harold, *The City and the Tsar.* Doubleday, 1948.
Manning, Clarence A., *The Story of the Ukraine.* Philosophical Library, 1947.
Mazour, Anatole, *Russia Past and Present.* Van Nostrand, 1951.
*Pares, Bernard, *A History of Russia.* Alfred A. Knopf, 1953.
†Raeff, Marc, ed., *Peter the Great: Reformer or Revolutionary?* D. C. Heath and Co., 1963.
Riasanovsky, Nicholas V., *A History of Russia.* Oxford University Press, 1963.
Riha, Thomas, ed., *Readings in Russian Civilization,* Vol. I, *Russia before Peter the Great 900-1700.* University of Chicago Press, 1964.
*Sumner, B. H., *Peter the Great and the Emergence of Russia.* Macmillan, 1951.
Tikhomirov, M., *The Towns of Ancient Rus.* Moscow, Foreign Languages Publishing House, 1959.
Vernadsky, George, *Bohdan, Hetman of the Ukraine.* Yale University Press, 1941.
Vernadsky, George, *A History of Russia.* 4 vols. Yale University Press, 1943-1959.
†Vernadsky, George, *A History of Russia.* 5th rev. ed. Yale University Press, 1961.
Vernadsky, George, transl., *Medieval Russian Laws.* Octagon Books Inc., 1965.
Vernadsky, George, *The Origins of Russia.* Oxford University Press, 1959.
Voyce, Arthur, *Moscow and the Roots of Russian Culture.* University of Oklahoma Press, 1964.
*Walsh, Warren B., ed., *Readings in Russian History.* 3 vols. Syracuse University Press, 1963.

LITERATURE AND CULTURE

Billington, James H., *The Icon and the Axe.* Alfred A. Knopf, 1966.
Chadwick, N. Kershaw, *Russian Heroic Poetry.* Russell & Russell, 1964.
Cherniavsky, Michael, *Tsar and People.* Yale University Press, 1961.
Chizhevskii, Dimitri, *History of Russian Literature.* The Hague, Mouton & Co., 1960.
Cross, Samuel H., and O. P. Sherbowitz-Wetzor, eds. and transls., *The Russian Primary Chronicle, Laurentian Text.* The Mediaeval Academy of America, 1953.
Gogol, Nikolai, *Taras Bulba.* Transl. by Andrew R. MacAndrew. A Signet Book, 1962.
†Gorer, Geoffrey, and John Rickman, *The People of Great Russia: A Psychological Study.* W. W. Norton, 1962.
Gudzii, Nikolai K., *A History of Early Russian Literature.* Transl. by Susan W. Jones. Macmillan, 1949.
Howe, Sonia E., *Some Russian Heroes, Saints and Sinners.* J. B. Lippincott, 1917.
*Miliukov, Paul, *Outline of Russian Culture.* Transl. by Valentine Ughet and Eleanor Davis. University of Pennsylvania Press, 1948.
Muchnic, Helen, *An Introduction to Russian Literature.* Doubleday, 1947.
†Nabokov, Vladimir, transl., *The Song of Igor's Campaign, An Epic of the Twelfth Century.* Vintage Books, 1960.
†Raeff, Marc, *Origins of the Russian Intelligentsia.* Harcourt, Brace & World, 1966.
Sokolov, Y. M., *Russian Folklore.* Macmillan, 1950.
†Weidle, Vladimir, *Russia Absent and Present.* Vintage Books, 1961.

Wiener, Leo, *Anthology of Russian Literature.* 2 vols. G. P. Putnam's Sons, 1902.
*Zenkovsky, Serge A., ed. and transl., *Medieval Russia's Epics, Chronicles, and Tales.* E. P. Dutton, 1963. (Source for excerpt from *The Lay of Igor's Campaign,* page 141.)

RELIGION

†Benz, Ernst, *The Eastern Orthodox Church.* Transl. by Richard and Clara Winston. Doubleday Anchor Books, 1963.
*Fedotov, George P., *The Russian Religious Mind.* 2 vols. Harvard University Press, 1966.
†Fedotov, George P., ed., *A Treasury of Russian Spirituality.* Harper Torchbooks, 1950.
French, Reginald Michael, *The Eastern Orthodox Church.* London, Hutchinson University Library, 1964.
Iswolsky, Helene, *Christ in Russia.* Bruce Publishing Company, 1960.
Meyendorff, John, *The Orthodox Church.* Transl. by John Chapin. Pantheon Books, 1962.
†Ware, Timothy, *The Orthodox Church.* Penguin Books, 1964.

ART AND ARCHITECTURE

Bunt, Cyril G. E., *A History of Russian Art.* The Studio, 1946.
Duncan, David Douglas, *The Kremlin.* New York Graphic Society, 1960.
Hamilton, George H., *The Art and Architecture of Russia.* Penguin Books, 1954.
Hare, Richard, *The Art and Artists of Russia.* London, Methuen & Co., Ltd., 1965.
Holme, Charles, ed., *Peasant Art in Russia.* The Studio, 1912.
Kondakov, N. P., *The Russian Icon.* Transl. by Ellis Minns. Oxford University Press, 1927.
Lasareff, Victor, and Otto Demus, *USSR Early Russian Icons.* Paris, New York Graphic Society by arrangement with UNESCO, 1958.
Onasch, Konrad, *Icons.* Transl. by Marianne von Herzfeld. A. S. Barnes and Company, 1963.
Ouspensky, Leonid, and Vladimir Lossky. *The Meaning of Icons.* Boston Book and Art Shop, 1952.
*Rice, Tamara Talbot, *A Concise History of Russian Art.* Frederick A. Praeger, 1963.
Rice, Tamara Talbot, *Russian Icons.* London, Spring Books, 1963.
Rybakov, B. A., ed., *Treasures in the Kremlin.* London, Paul Hamlyn, 1964.
Voronin, N. N., ed., *Palaces and Churches of the Kremlin.* London, Paul Hamlyn, 1965.
Voyce, Arthur, *The Moscow Kremlin: Its History, Architecture, and Art Treasures.* University of California Press, 1954.

CONTEMPORARY ACCOUNTS

Anderson, M. S., *Britain's Discovery of Russia.* London, Macmillan, 1958.
Bond, Edward A., ed., *Russia at the Close of the Sixteenth Century (Of the Russe Common Wealth* by Dr. Giles Fletcher, and *The Travels* of Sir Jerome Horsey). Hakluyt Society Series No. 20. Burt Franklin, 1964.
Fennell, J.L.I., ed. and transl., *The Correspondence Between Prince A. M. Kurbsky and Tsar Ivan IV of Russia, 1564-1579.* Cambridge University Press, 1963.
Glaser, F. L., ed., *Scenes from the Court of Peter the Great* (Based on the Latin Diary of Johann G. Korb). Nicholas L. Brown, 1921.
Haxthausen, Baron von, *The Russian Empire.* Transl. by Robert Farie. 2 vols. London, Chapman and Hall, 1856.
Leroy-Beaulieu, Anatole, *The Empire of the Tsars.* Transl. by Z. Ragozin. 2 vols. G. P. Putnam's Sons, 1898.
Major, R. H., ed. and transl., *Notes Upon Russia (Rerum Moscoviticarum Commentarii* by Sigismund von Herberstein). Hakluyt Society Series No. 10 and 12. 2 vols. Burt Franklin, 1963.
Marsden, William, transl., *The Travels of Marco Polo.* Dell Publishing Co., 1961.
Morgan, E. Delmar, and C. H. Coote, eds., *Early Voyages and Travels to Russia and Persia* (Anthony Jenkinson and other Englishmen), Vol. II. Hakluyt Society Series No. 73. Burt Franklin, 1965.
Putnam, Peter, ed., *Seven Britons in Imperial Russia, 1698-1812.* Princeton University Press, 1952.

ART INFORMATION AND PICTURE CREDITS

The sources for the illustrations in this book are set forth below. Descriptive notes on the works of art are included. Credits for pictures positioned from left to right are separated by semicolons, from top to bottom by dashes. Photographers' names that follow a descriptive note appear in parentheses. Abbreviations include "c" for century and "ca" for circa.

Cover—Detail of cupolas, Church of the Transfiguration, Kizhi Island, wood, 1714 (Erich Lessing from Magnum). 8-9—Map by Leo and Diane Dillon.

CHAPTER 1: 10—Long-toothed comb decorated with Scythian warriors from royal tomb at Solokha in the Dnieper Valley, gold, 5th c. B.C., courtesy State Hermitage Museum, Leningrad (James Whitmore). 12-13—Map by Rafael D. Palacios. 15—Four-faced idol, stone, 1000-500 B.C. (Novosti Press Agency, Moscow). 16-17—Petroglyphs found near Lake Onega, ca. 1000 B.C. (Novosti from Sovfoto, New York). 19—Map by Rafael D. Palacios. 21-29—Illuminations from the Radziwill Chronicle, 15th c., courtesy Academy of Sciences, Leningrad (Erich Lessing from Magnum).

CHAPTER 2: 30—Helmet of Prince Yaroslav Vsevolodovich, hammered iron ornamented with silver gilt repoussé work, early 13th c., courtesy The Armoury of the Kremlin, Moscow (Karel Neubert, courtesy Artia, Prague). 34—Tally of collector of princely custom duties from the state of Kiev, wood, 11th c. (Novosti Press Agency, Moscow). 36-37—Drawing by Victor Lazzaro. 41—Church of Lazarus, Kizhi Island, wood, 14th c. (Erich Lessing from Magnum).

42-43—View of cupolas of Church of the Transfiguration, wood, 1714, and Pokrovskaya Church, wood, 1764, Kizhi Island; view of cupolas of Church of the Transfiguration, Kizhi Island, wood, 1714 (Erich Lessing from Magnum). 44—Door of the iconostasis and detail, Church of the Transfiguration, Kizhi Island, gilded wood, mid-18th c. (Erich Lessing from Magnum). 45—Cross from the Church of the Transfiguration, Kizhi Island, wood, 1737 (Erich Lessing from Magnum). 46-47—House of Oshevnev and detail, Kizhi Island, originally from Bolshoy Klimetskiy, wood, 1876 (Erich Lessing from Magnum). 48-49—Woodcarvings from house from Upper Volga region, 2nd half of 19th c., courtesy State Historical Museum, Moscow (Erich Lessing from Magnum). 50-51—Beehive from village of Timirevo, wood, late 19th c., courtesy State Historical Museum, Moscow; interior of Oshevnev house, Kizhi Island, 1876; wooden mug from Trans-Baikol area, 19th c., courtesy State Historical Museum, Moscow; starling houses in the form of a man and a woman from village of Timirevo, wood, late 19th c., courtesy State Historical Museum, Moscow—wooden bowl from northern Russia, 1819, courtesy State Historical Museum, Moscow (Erich Lessing from Magnum). 52-53—Spinning distaffs, wood, 19th c., courtesy State Historical Museum, Moscow (Erich Lessing from Magnum).

CHAPTER 3: 54—Mongol Tartar from *Scenes Among the Mongol Tartars: the Captivity of Ts'ai Wen Chi,* detail from a handscroll, ink on paper, Ming Dynasty 14th-15th c., courtesy Freer Gallery of Art, Washington, D.C. 57—Mongol coin, 1403 (Novosti from Sovfoto, New York). 59—Map by Rafael D. Palacios. 63—Drawing from *Rerum Moscoviticarum Commentarii* by Sigismund von Herberstein, 1571, courtesy Cracow University Library, Poland (Bohdan Walknowski, Cracow). 65—Drawing by Arno Sternglass. 66-75—Paintings by Apolinari Vasnetsov, early 20th c., courtesy Picture Gallery of White Russia, Minsk, Museum of the History and Reconstruction of Moscow, Moscow, State Historical Museum, Moscow, State Tretyakov Gallery, Moscow and Private Collections (Novosti Press Agency, Moscow).

CHAPTER 4: 76—Portrait of Ivan the Terrible by Mikhail Gerasimov, gypsum, 1964, courtesy State Historical Museum, Moscow (Novosti Press Agency, Moscow). 80—Illustration from *Chronique Remezov* by Semen Remezov, ca. 1700 (H. Roger Viollet, Paris). 85—Interior view, Monastery of the Holy Trinity, Zagorsk, 16th c. (Cornell Capa from Magnum). 86-87—Panagia or medallion, cameo carved on onyx, 12th c., with gold setting of jewels, pearls and colored enamel, 16th c., courtesy The Armoury of the Kremlin, Moscow (Karel Neubert, courtesy Artia, Prague)—vestment of Patriarch Nikon, brocade, 1654, courtesy The Armoury of the Kremlin, Moscow (Karel Neubert, courtesy Artia, Prague); interior view, Monastery of the Holy Trinity, Zagorsk, 16th c. (Cornell Capa from Magnum). 88-89—Interior view, Monastery of the Holy Trinity, Zagorsk, 16th c. (Cornell Capa from Magnum); processional cross, wood, Novgorod School, ca. 1500, courtesy George R. Hann Collection (Robert S. Crandall). 90-91—Cover of *Manuscript Gospel,* gold, transparent and opaque enamels, emeralds, sapphires and rubies, 1678, courtesy The Armoury of the Kremlin, Moscow (Karel Neubert, courtesy Artia, Prague)—detail from above; interior view, Monastery of the Holy Trinity, Zagorsk, 16th c. (Cornell Capa from Magnum). 92—Interior view, Monastery of the Holy Trinity, Zagorsk, 16th c. (Cornell Capa from Magnum); chalice, gold ornamented with enamels, emeralds, rubies, sapphires and diamonds, 1664, courtesy The Armoury of the Kremlin, Moscow (Karel Neubert, courtesy Artia, Prague). 93—Interior view, Monastery of the Holy Trinity, Zagorsk, 16th c. (Cornell Capa from Magnum).

CHAPTER 5: 94—Detail from *The Boyarina Morozova* by Vasili Ivanovich Surikov, oil on canvas, 1887, courtesy State Tretyakov Gallery, Moscow (Erich Lessing from Magnum). 97—*Palm Sunday Procession* from pictures collected by Augustin Freyherr von Meyerberg, 1661-1662 (Ullstein Bilderdienst, Berlin-Tempelhof). 101—Diagram from *The Meaning of Icons* by Leonid Ouspensky and Vladimir Lossky, courtesy Boston Book and Art Shop, 1952. 103—*Our Lady of Vladimir* by an icon painter of Andrei Rublev's circle, tempera on wood panel, early 15th c., Cathedral of the Assumption, Kremlin, Moscow (Karel Neubert, courtesy Artia, Prague). 104—*St. Demetrios,* mosaic, late 11th c., courtesy State Tretyakov Gallery, Moscow (Novosti Press Agency, Moscow). 105—*St. George,* icon of Novgorod School, tempera on wood panel, late 15th c., courtesy George R. Hann Collection (Robert S. Crandall). 106-107—Detail from *Icon of the Prophet Elijah,* tempera on wood panel, early 18th c., courtesy Ikonen-Museum, Recklinghausen, Germany (Walter Sanders). 108-109—Center: *Annunciation,* icon from Royal Doors from Novgorod, tempera on wood panel, 1450, courtesy George R. Hann Collection (Robert S. Crandall). Left and below: *Nativity,* icon of Novgorod School, ca. 1400, courtesy George R. Hann Collection (Robert S. Crandall)—*Baptism of Christ,* icon of Novgorod School, tempera on wood panel, 16th c., courtesy Ikonen-Museum, Recklinghausen, Germany (Walter Sanders); *Transfiguration,* icon of Novgorod School, tempera on wood panel, 1500, courtesy George R. Hann Collection (Robert S. Crandall); *Raising of Lazarus,* icon of Moscow School, tempera on wood panel, 15th c., courtesy George R. Hann Collection (Robert S. Crandall); *Crucifixion,* icon of Vladimir-Suzdal School, tempera on wood panel, ca. 1500, courtesy The Walters Art Gallery, Baltimore (Henry Beville); *Resurrection,* icon of Novgorod School, tempera on wood panel, 14th c., courtesy George R. Hann Collection (Robert S. Crandall); *Ascension,* icon of Moscow School with Novgorod traits, tempera on wood panel, 16th c., courtesy George R. Hann Collection (Robert S. Crandall). 110—*Archangel Michael,* icon by Andrei Rublev, tempera on wood panel, ca. 1407, courtesy State Tretyakov Gallery, Moscow (Novosti Press Agency, Moscow). *Archangel Gabriel,* icon of Novgorod School, tempera on wood panel, 14th c., courtesy George R. Hann Collection (Robert S. Crandall). 112—*St. Nicholas Saves Storm-Tossed Sailors,* detail from icon of Novgorod School, tempera on wood panel, late 16th c., courtesy Ikonen-Museum, Recklinghausen, Germany (Walter Sanders). 113—*St. Nicholas and His Life,* icon of Novgorod School, tempera on wood panel, ca. 1500, courtesy George R. Hann Collection (Robert S. Crandall).

CHAPTER 6: 114—Throne of Ivan the Terrible, wood covered with ivory plates, 16th c., courtesy The Armoury of the Kremlin, Moscow (Novosti Press Agency, Moscow). 119—View of Czar's palace in 17th c., drawing by Potapov from *An Essay of Ancient Russian Civil Architecture,* 1902, courtesy State Historical Museum, Moscow (Novosti Press Agency, Moscow). 120—Coat of Arms of Czar Alexis Mikhailovich, 1667 (Novosti Press Agency, Moscow). 123—*Rurik* (Historia-Photo, Bad Sachsa). 124-125—Portraits of Oleg, Igor and Olga from *Ancient Russian History,* engravings by Pierre Chenu, 17th c., courtesy Cabinet des Estampes Bibliothèque Nationale, Paris (Photo Bulloz, Paris); *Yaroslav the Wise* by Mikhail Gerasimov, courtesy State Historical Museum, Moscow (Novosti Press Agency, Moscow); *Vladimir* (Culver Pictures, New York)—*Cyril and Methodius* (Interfoto MTI, Budapest). 126—Genghis Khan, courtesy Museum of Ulan Bator, Mongolia (Interfoto MTI, Budapest); *Batu Khan,* woodcut, courtesy Cracow University Library, Poland (Bohdan Walknowski, Cracow). 127—*Alexander Nevsky,* mural, 17th c., Cathedral of the Archangel Michael, Moscow (Novosti Press Agency, Moscow)—*Ivan I,* drawing from Portraits, *Coat-of-Arms and Seals of the Grand State Book,* 1672, State Historical Museum, Moscow (Novosti Press Agency, Moscow)—*Dimitry Donskoy,* mural, 17th c., Cathedral of the Archangel Michael, Moscow (Novosti Press Agency, Moscow); *Tamerlane* by Mikhail Gerasimov, courtesy State Historical Museum, Moscow (Novosti Press Agency, Moscow). 128-129—*Ivan III* from *Portraits of Moscow Rulers* by Rovinsky, 1882, courtesy Museum of the History and the Reconstruction of Moscow (Novosti Press Agency, Moscow); *Czar Fedor,* courtesy State Historical Museum, Moscow (Novosti Press Agency, Moscow); *Boris Godunov,* courtesy Museum of the History and Reconstruction of Moscow, Moscow (Novosti Press Agency, Moscow); *Dimitry, son of Ivan IV,* courtesy Bibliothèque Nationale, Paris (Photo Bulloz, Paris)—*False Dimitry I* by Polish painter of 17th c., courtesy State Historical Museum, Moscow (Novosti Press Agency, Moscow); Patriarch Philaret, 17th c., courtesy State Historical Museum, Moscow (Novosti Press Agency, Moscow). 130-131—*Bohdan Khmelnitsky,* engraving, 1666, courtesy Cracow University Library, Cracow (Bohdan Walknowski, Cracow); *Patriarch Nikon* from Meierberg Album, courtesy State Historical Museum, Moscow (Novosti Press Agency, Moscow); *Sophie the Regent* (Ullstein Bilderdienst, Berlin-Tempelhof); *Czar Alexis and his wife Natalia,* medal commemorating the birth of Peter the Great, 1672 (Novosti Press Agency, Moscow)—*Eudoxia Lopukhina,* engraving, courtesy State Hermitage Museum, Leningrad (Novosti Press Agency, Moscow).

CHAPTER 7: 132—Illustration from *Les Peuples de la Russie,* volume I, *Nations Composant l'Empire Russe* by Karl, Graf von Rechberg und Rothenlowen, hand-colored engraving, 1812, courtesy Library of Congress, Rare Book Department, Washington, D.C. 134-135—Decorative edge of bedspread embroidered on handmade netting and drawn thread linen, from St. Petersburg, 18th c., courtesy Brooklyn Museum of Art, New York (Lee Boltin). 137—Boyar costume, 17th c. (Radio Times Hulton Picture Library, London). 139—Façade of palace at Versailles, France, 17th c. (Pierre Boulat). 143-153—Illustrations from *A Picturesque Representation of the Manners, Customs and Amusements of the Russians* by John Augustus Atkinson and James Walker, colored etchings, 1803-1804, London, Courtesy of The Free Library of Philadelphia, The Rare Book Department, Philadelphia (Robert S. Crandall).

CHAPTER 8: 154—*Peter the Great* by M. V. Lomonosov, mosaic, 1755, courtesy State Hermitage Museum, Leningrad (Erich Lessing from Magnum). 156—Beard Licenses, ca. 1725 (Novosti Press Agency, Moscow). 158—Cartoon, ca. 1725 (Radio Times Hulton Picture Library, London). 161—Page from newspaper, November 30, 1723, courtesy Library of Congress, Rare Book Department, Washington, D.C. 162—Map by Rafael D. Palacios. 165—View of domes of Cathedral of the Archangel Michael and Ivan the Great Belfry, Kremlin, Moscow, 1505-1508 (John Bryson). 166-167—Metropolitan's chair in Cathedral of the Archangel, Kremlin, Moscow, white stone, 1505-1508 (Karel Neubert, courtesy Artia, Prague); interior view of Church of the Nativity of Our Lady, Kremlin, Moscow, stone, 1393 (Karel Neubert, courtesy Artia, Prague). 168—Interior view of Cathedral of the Assumption, Kremlin, Moscow, built 1474-1479 with murals by Aristotle Fioravante, 1642-1643 (Karel Neubert, courtesy Artia, Prague). 169—West portal of Cathedral of the Annunciation, Kremlin, Moscow, cathedral built 1485-1489, portal built ca. 1560 (Karel Neubert, courtesy Artia, Prague)—interior view of Cathedral of the Annunciation, Kremlin, Moscow, built 1485-1489, murals done in 1505 (Karel Neubert, courtesy Artia, Prague). 170-171—Interior view of Terem Palace, Kremlin, Moscow, built 1635-1636 (Karel Neubert, courtesy Artia, Prague); exterior of St. Basil's Cathedral, Red Square, Moscow, built 1560 (Stan Wayman)—interior view of Terem Palace, Kremlin, Moscow, built 1635-1636 (Karel Neubert, courtesy Artia, Prague). 172-173—View of Peterhof fountains, Leningrad, allegorical representation of the Volkhov River (Colin Jones); view of Peterhof fountains, Leningrad, Naiad with Tritons and Samson in background (Jerry Cooke).

ACKNOWLEDGMENTS

The editors of the book are particularly indebted to Harvey L. Dyck, Associate Professor of History, University of Toronto, who served as overall consultant, and to Julian Biddle of Northwestern University's Russian Department, who translated the Church Slavonic text for "The Tales of Bygone Years." The editors also wish to thank the Rev. John Meyendorff, St. Vladimir's Orthodox Theological Seminary; Dr. Eric C. Hulmer, Harmony, Pennsylvania; George R. Hann Collection, Sewickley Heights, Pennsylvania; Mrs. Svetlana Umrichin, Nyack, N.Y.; Professor Ihor Ševčenko, Professor of Byzantine History and Literature and Director of Studies at the Dumbarton Oaks Center for Byzantine Studies; Moscow Kremlin Museums; State Historical Museum, Moscow; State Hermitage Museum, Leningrad; State Tretyakov Gallery, Moscow; State Russian Museum, Leningrad; Museum of the History and Reconstruction of the City of Moscow, Moscow; Museum of History, Leningrad; Russian Folk Art Museum, Moscow; Central Naval Museum, Leningrad; Army Historical Museum, Leningrad; Vasnetsov Memorial House, Moscow; State Museum of Russian Architecture, Moscow; Architectural Museum of U.S.S.R. Academy of Construction and Architecture, Moscow; House of Peter First, Leningrad; Trude Beckova, Art Centrum, Prague; Hans-Heinric Richter, Deutsche Fotothek, Dresden; Heinz Skrobucha, Ikonen Museum, Recklinghausen; Hirmer Verlag, Munich; Staatsbibliothek, Berlin; Wilfried Göpel, Archiv Fuer Kunst und Geschichte, Berlin; Ettore lo Gatto, Accademia Nazionale dei Lincei, Rome; Oreste Toutzevitch, Bibliothécaire Spécialiste, Bibliothèque Nationale, Paris; Simon Beliz, collector of Russian art, Paris; Department of Oriental Printed Books and Manuscripts, British Museum, London; Department of Manuscripts, British Museum, London.

INDEX